The Hasidic Parable

THE HASIDIC PARABLE

Aryeh Wineman

The Jewish Publication Society
Philadelphia
2001 • 5761

Cover Art by Baruch Nachshon
Composition by Sasgen Graphic Design
Design by Sasgen Graphic Design
Manufactured in the United States of America

09 08 07 06 05 04 03 02 01   10 9 8 7 6 5 4 3 2 1

            Library of Congress Cataloging-inPublication Data

Wineman, Aryeh.
    The Hasidic parable / Aryeh Wineman.
    p. cm.
    Includes 40 parables translated from Hebrew.
    Includes bibliographical references.
    ISBN 0-8276-0707-5
    1. Hasidic parables. 2. Hasidic parables--History and criticism. 1. Title.

    BM532.W46 2001
    296.1'9 21; aa05 12-07--dc00   00-067287

In memory of my parents

CONTENTƒ

Preface

〜

After examining narrative dimensions of earlier phases of Jewish mysticism, I was drawn to the hasidic parable as a logical continuation of my previous research and writing. This book is the natural culmination of my immersion over the past several years in a study of the parables. While seeking to clarify their meaning as well as the historical and literary significance and concepts inherent in them, I also became interested in the nature of the genre of the hasidic parable itself.

I hope that I have been able to cast some light upon the parables in this collection and perhaps upon the phenomenon of the hasidic parable. I have tried to convey to the reader my own appreciation for many of the parables included in this volume along with the preciousness of the spiritual core of Hasidism's worldview and of its value system. The hasidic legacy is an indispensable key in the quest for a spirituality rooted in Jewish sources, and in discovering an inwardness and depth often overlooked in more conventional expressions of Jewish teaching.

An examination of some of the parables found in the classical hasidic texts reveals spiritual directions that might have become lost in the context of Hasidism's historical hostility toward modernity throughout much of the nineteenth and twentieth centuries. The parables convey that beyond the facade of contemporary institutional Hasidism and its cultural identification with the past, the very core of its teaching is soulfulness itself.

I wish to thank the editors of *Judaism, Hebrew Studies,* and *Prooftexts: A Journal of Jewish Literary History* for permission to draw upon studies I've written that first appeared in those journals.

I am grateful for opportunities to present papers relevant to the subject of this book at conferences of the Association for Jewish Studies and the

National Association of Professors of Hebrew. I would also like to thank my congregation for affording me the opportunity to utilize the resources of the National Library in Jerusalem and the Gershom Scholem Center there in order to complete my research for this project.

My appreciation to Dr. Ellen Frankel, editor-in-chief of The Jewish Publication Society, for her interest and encouragement in this project, and to Carol Hupping, managing editor, and editor Sam Cardillo for all their assistance in preparing my manuscript for publication. ◆

—**Aryeh Wineman**
Troy, New York
Fall, 1999

Introduction

⌣

*W*hen one thinks of Hasidism—the Jewish pietist movement that emerged in the eighteenth century in the Carpathian Mountains of the Ukraine and spread with remarkable rapidity among a large sector of Eastern European Jewry—certain basic cultural associations almost immediately come to mind. Among them is parable. An impressive array of striking parables can be found in texts from Hasidism's classical period, from the late eighteenth through the early nineteenth centuries. One does not find parables in all hasidic texts from this period; some have none, some provide very few examples, while still other texts, including some of the basic collections of homilies from Hasidism's most creative period, abound with parables.

The most basic definition of parable is an imaginative story whose meaning refers to something quite beyond itself; it alludes to an analogy or application not contained within the story proper. A parable is a work of fiction, necessarily brief and compact, which is not told for its own sake, but to make a point and speak a truth.

The phenomenon of parable has its roots in oral tradition and folk literature, and the prevalence of parables in many of the classical hasidic texts testifies to the oral context of hasidic teaching. In earlier stages of Jewish mystic tradition, teachings were essentially transmitted via written texts; authors and students of such texts may never have shared any geographical proximity or engaged one another face-to-face. In sharp contrast, Hasidism functioned as a circle of mystics and their students, and later as communities comprising a definite social context. Consequently hasidic teaching was articulated and transmitted orally in a setting of students or followers who heard, rather than read, the master's discourse,[1] and this naturally fostered the creation of parables.

As a literary genre, the parable was known as far back as the ancient world, where examples in the Bible, in the Christian Gospels, and in talmudic and midrashic texts all testify to the flourishing of parable as a rhetorical form. (Throughout this book, Talmud references are referred to as follows: Babylonian Talmud is B., for example, B. Pe'ah, and Jerusalem Talmud is J., as in J. Pe'ah.) Such ancient sources, in turn, inspired the use of parable in later Jewish and Christian preaching and also in medieval philosophical and kabbalistic texts. Parable is common also in the mystic teachings of other religious traditions, including Islamic mysticism (Sufism) and Zen Buddhism. Even the opponents of the emerging hasidic stream employed parables, as is evident most notably in those of Ya'akov ben Ze'ev Krantz, known as the Dubno Maggid.[2]

Hasidism, however, gave new life to the parable form. Compared with examples found either in various earlier sources or in texts contemporary with emerging Hasidism, many parables found in the teachings of the hasidic masters possess extraordinary vitality and literary power. And while any number of parables within those same hasidic texts might seem quite conventional, an impressive number of them stand out. When a modern author—such as the late Hebrew writer Shmuel Yosef Agnon— interwove in his stories his own original examples of the hasidic parable, he sought the kind of ambience and qualities found precisely in those more unconventional examples.

Qualities of the Hasidic Parable

Among those traits characterizing the hasidic parable is the thoroughly unexpected turn, jarring the reader's (or listener's) expectations. Sometimes the surprise element that awakens the reader is the mood created in the parable, or it might be the story itself, or the accompanying explanation or explication of the parable.

Parables found in homiletical compositions of the pre-hasidic or non-hasidic Jewish world of Eastern Europe[3] often appear wordy and drawn out in contrast to the much more compact texture of the hasidic parable. Moreover, the former rarely contain any element of the unexpected, within the story or in its application. Upon beginning to read the parables in such texts, the reader already perceives exactly how the story will unfold and grasps its meaning. In contrast, the surprise element of the hasidic parable is one of its key characteristics.

Surprise is not unrelated to paradox. And while the brevity of the parable form naturally invites a paradoxical nuance, the hasidic parable frequently raises that implicit potential for paradox to a higher pitch. Even the famous parables of the Dubno Maggid, ingeniously crafted to parallel a stated situation, generally lack those qualities of surprise and paradox found in the hasidic parable. With eighteenth-century Hasidism, the parable form often transcended its more conventional nature to incorporate qualities present in earlier Jewish mystic texts and in tales included in the kabbalistic ethical texts of the preceding centuries.[4]

The Structure of the Hasidic Parable

The hasidic parable continued the bipartite structure of the earlier rabbinic parable (found in the Talmud and Midrash) consisting of the *mashal*—the parable story itself—and the *nimshal*—the application or significance of the story as supplied by the teller of the parable.[5] It also contained parables revolving around a king, a staple in the classical rabbinic parable, although the roles of the father and the teacher also became recurrent figures in hasidic parables. Both the general form of the rabbinic parable and the convention of the king-*mashal* served to lend the hasidic parable a traditional ambience, even when the familiar and traditional literary form might conceal a highly innovative and sometimes even radical point of view vis-à-vis the more generally accepted mode of traditional Jewish teaching.

In other, perhaps more significant, ways, the hasidic parable did not follow the example of the classical rabbinic parable. Whereas in midrashic literature the parable generally served an exegetical function, supporting a particular reading of a biblical verse,[6] this is not the case with the hasidic parable.

To define the function of the hasidic parable, one must focus on the structure of those parables that have the greatest literary power and the most profound import. The reader can often detect in the most memorable hasidic parables a kind of a priori premise presented as a logical or prevalent way of thinking. That initial premise might be spelled out explicitly although even when it is not, it is fairly evident. The parable then challenges and even negates that premise in favor of another very different way of understanding. The parable leads the reader to regard that a priori premise as a surface perception and to consider an alternative view as approaching the very same subject with significantly greater depth and insight.

Such a structure in itself is not a hasidic innovation. In fact, a highly illuminating example of this kind of parable structure can be found that antedates Hasidism by almost five centuries. In a well-known parable from the Zohar—a medieval mystic text which became the basic text of Kabbalah, the predominant Jewish mystic tradition—a king sends his son away to a village so that there he might grow to be capable of learning the ways of the royal palace. Later, realizing that his son has matured, the king sends the boy's mother to bring their son back to the palace. The king represents God; the mother, the Shekhinah (the distinctly feminine member of the configuration of *sefirot,* manifestations of the Divine); while the son is the higher holy soul temporarily sent to this world, which is likened to a village:

> Nevertheless, it is the way of the world that we villagers weep with the departure of the king's son. One wise person who was there, however, asked us, "Why are you weeping? Is he not the king's son? It is not fitting then that he continue to live among us, for his true place is in his father's palace."

> Were the righteous and wise to grasp this, they would instead rejoice on that day when it is time for one to depart and ascend from this world, for is it not an honor for a person that the Matron [the Shekhinah] comes for him to bring him to the Royal Palace that the King might thereupon rejoice with him day after day?[7]

Rabbinic parables sometimes contrast the responses of the wise and the foolish. In a talmudic parable, for example, a king invites his servants to a feast without indicating when the feast will take place, and the two groups respond very differently. The foolish do not prepare until the actual time of the feast is announced, whereas the wise are in a state of perpetual readiness. When the feast (representing death) is suddenly announced, the foolish have no time to prepare.[8] The reader naturally casts the foolish in a critical light and identifies with the wise. In the zoharic parable cited above, however, it is understood that the reader initially identifies with the more "normal" view of death as an occasion of sadness; the wise man in the story represents a challenging viewpoint, which radically negates the villagers' and the reader's a priori premise. This zoharic parable of death might serve as a kind of prototype of the later hasidic parable, and many of the parables in this collection share its basic structure.

That structure lends the parable a distinctly polemical quality, even though the parables were addressed to the hasidic master's own students or followers, who were disposed to accept his teachings. The initial premises of such hasidic parables are sometimes identified with attitudes representing the accepted ideals of Jewish religious life in Eastern Europe as the hasidic masters perceived them and criticized them. The structure of those hasidic parables makes possible a transformation of thinking. It alters the reader's understanding in favor of an alternate and higher conception of the nature of religious life and of his relationship to himself, to God, and to the world.

This kind of literary structure testifies to Hasidism's essentially unconventional spiritual consciousness, characteristic of its earlier period. That core structure of the hasidic parable suggests that Hasidism's own strong and natural identification with Jewish tradition and traditional Jewish society conceals its own radical transformation of that tradition as it was conventionally understood.

In this way the hasidic parable can be likened to a guide directing a person from a lower level of understanding and awareness to a higher level. This is the case in numerous instances of simple analogy as well as in parables with more complex narrative content. In both, the analogy serves as a lens through which one can view a given subject in a strikingly different light, and the goal of the parable is nothing less than a metamorphosis of one's understanding. The initial a priori premise is often so basic and pervasive in life that a statement suggesting an alternative view would fail to impress the listener. Only via the parable can one move beyond a conventional "commonsense" view to grasp an alternative, transcendent perspective. Parable, it would appear, played an essential role in Hasidism's liberating its followers from "conformed conception"—to quote Rachel Elior, a noted contemporary scholar of Hasidism.[9]

In a Yiddish folk parable[10] told in the name of the Maggid of Dubno, the naked Truth finds no acceptance and walks around rejected until Parable lends Truth its own beautifully colored garments. Then, in asso-

ciation with Parable, Truth finds favor in everyone's eyes. This folktale
perceives parable as the embellishment of an idea, making a point more
striking and appealing, even though the truth itself, while lacking the
same appeal, would nevertheless make sense if stated independently of
the parable.

In references to the nature of parable found scattered in hasidic texts,
one finds the contrasting idea that truth can sometimes be understood
only by means of parable. "Without the parable, [the listener] would neither grasp the idea nor accept it, due to its distance from common reasoning, and for this same reason the person did not accept the idea prior
to hearing the parable."[11]

Not infrequently in hasidic texts, the reader notes the comment: "In
order to draw something nearer to the mind, we employ a parable."[12] A
parable can sometimes be an indispensable tool in enabling readers to
comprehend what they would otherwise not fathom. In this vein, Yitzhak
of Radvil explained that, paradoxically, only through the concrete garb or
covering provided by an analogy can one grasp the more abstract idea
conveyed in the parable,[13] just as the human eye can gaze at the bright
sun only through a curtain or veil.[14]

A parable is not a logical argument. Like any analogy, a parable accentuates certain similarities while glossing over potentially crucial differences.[15] But even if the hasidic parable does not logically prove its thesis,
it does achieve something else. It entices the mind to entertain the possibility of a different perspective on its subject. It subtly expands the para-
meters of the mind, and in the process one's beliefs about reality, life, the
cosmos, God, and self are open to change.[16]

The Hasidic Homily

The hasidic parable was told as part of a larger discourse, namely the
hasidic homily (*derash*). Through the sermon or lecture, the hasidic master generally interpreted a verse or passage from the Torah or occasionally from another part of Scripture. The homily, as it has come down in
its written form, consists of notes on the actual oral lecture or sermon or
as a summary or outline of the actual homily as it was delivered. The
homily was generally delivered on Shabbat, either at the Friday evening
gathering around the table (*tisch*) or at the Shabbat afternoon Third Meal

(*se'udah shelishit*), and any attempt to record or summarize the discourse in writing would not occur at least until after the conclusion of the Shabbat. Those notes or summaries of homilies, though hardly identical with the actual sermon as delivered, comprise the only available source for the classical hasidic parables that have come down to us.

The very first hasidic text to be printed, *Toledot Ya'akov Yosef,* by Rabbi Ya'akov Yosef of Polonnoye, printed in 1780, is a collection of such homilies on the weekly Torah portions. It was followed by a steady stream of collections of homilies by other hasidic teachers, including many of the students of the Maggid, Dov Baer of Mezherich, who placed his indelible stamp on classical hasidic thought.

One might think of the homily as the ore from which the parable is extracted. That analogy, however helpful, nevertheless misses the mark. For one thing, one cannot really extract a parable from its context within the homily, and for this reason, whenever possible, I have tried in this collection to take note of a parable's textual context within the homily. In addition, the analogy of homily as ore might suggest that the homily itself has no value apart from the parable found within it, whereas the hasidic homily is important in its own right, both as the essential literary source of hasidic teaching and as an often remarkably creative interpretation of a hallowed text. While the hasidic homily is most often occasioned by a verse from the Torah, that verse is then read in the light of connotations and overtones that the teacher overhears in the text. Consequently, the very subject of a homily is invariably situated at a pronounced distance from the plain meaning of the Torah passage. The hasidic master's reading of the sacred text through the lens of hasidic values and themes is sometimes nothing less than ingenious.

Through associations of words drawn from earlier sources or from hasidic thought itself, the homily deepens and transforms the meaning of the Torah passage, voicing what the master believed to be the inner, deeper meaning of that text. Essentially, the hasidic homily understands the text of the Torah as a code for Hasidism's own approach to the worship of God in its most comprehensive sense and for its basic attitudes toward life, self, and God.[17] The Torah and its every word are read as allusions to hasidic values, with their emphasis upon inwardness and depth of devotion, upon the goal of an inner attachment to God in one's whole life, and upon a sense of the Divine as ever present in life. In its particular grasp of the Torah, the hasidic homily views the universe itself as a mere garment of the Divine, which underlies all being and which is ultimately the sole reality.

The collections of homilies by various hasidic teachers and masters are the sources of the parables we shall proceed to explore in this volume.

How the Hasidic Masters Viewed Parable

How did the hasidic masters understand the phenomenon of parable and its place in their homilies and teachings? Rabbi Ya'akov Yosef of Polonnoye remarked that a preacher seeking to influence his listeners to correct their ways should be aware that they have no driving desire to hear his message. And should he speak directly, they will close their minds and ears to his words. Hence, the necessity to sweeten them with parable and literary flourish. These are likened to wine and milk, which will draw listeners, unlike a more direct approach, likened to water.[18]

In another homily, the same Ya'akov Yosef of Polonnoye provides a medical parallel to the role of parable. Drawing upon a much older analogy, he recommends that a person suffering from a sick soul should be given milk or wine because water, which he really needs, tastes bitter to him, due to the nature of his illness. So while a healthy person hearing a discourse can imbibe directly its inner ethical or spiritual teaching (water), a morally weak person must instead imbibe image and parable— wine and milk, which nevertheless contain water, the teaching's inner content.[19] The parable, then, is an aid to understanding reality. In an ideal world there would be no need for parable (and in such an ideal world—to the mind of Ya'akov Yosef of Polonnoye—this book would never have been written!).

Others went even further to convey that the very nature of the human mind and of human existence mandate parable. In the words of Rabbi Levi Yitzhak of Berdichev, "Since it is necessary to take what is born in the kiss of the divine word and bring it closer to the human mind, we therefore draw upon parable and imagery that we might be able to understand the insights proceeding from a higher source."[20]

Levi Yitzhak's teacher, the Maggid, Dov Baer of Mezherich, provides us with an even more revealing approach toward parable. The Maggid (literally, "preacher"), who probably more than anyone else crystallized the worldview and character of classical hasidic thought, rose into prominence during the years following the death of the Baal Shem Tov in 1760, and until his own death twelve years later he attracted several students, who went on to establish hasidic communities over a fairly wide geographical area. The Maggid related parable to the principle of *tzimtzum* (contraction), a crucial concept in the kabbalistic teaching of the sixteenth-century mystic Rabbi Isaac Luria. In Lurianic Kabbalah, *tzimtzum* signifies a retreat on the part of the Divine from a part of its own infinite, unbounded state, making for an empty, primordial space in which a cosmos could ultimately emerge.[21] Many of the Maggid's parables, drawn from the world of interpersonal relationships, are presented as analogues to his own reinterpretation of that earlier kabbalistic concept in light of the essential hasidic premise that there is nothing in which the Divine is not present—not even the primordial space from which God retreated, as it were. In the thinking of the Maggid, *tzimtzum* was no longer a radical occurrence affecting the Divine; rather, it was either a contrived act rooted in the Divine Will to allow a cosmos to come into being or an appearance from the human side of the divine–human divide but one not affecting the Divine at all.

In some of his parables, the Maggid explained *tzimtzum* as analogous to a parent or teacher suppressing his own much higher level of intellect in order to relate to a young child. Similarly, the Maggid explained, God contracts Himself, as it were, in accordance with a person's capacity to grasp the Divine. A human being is able to grasp the greater divine reality not as it is in truth, but rather only in terms of God's vastly contracted presence to accommodate the limitations of human understanding in general, as well as the mental and spiritual limitations of individuals.[22]

A father wants to impart wisdom to his child, but the child is unable to grasp the depth of that wisdom, so the father has to bring the child to understand by means of a parable and in this way the child will be able to understand the wisdom. Considering this situation, we realize that the father himself is a wise man, capable of understanding without the need for a parable, which is superfluous for him. Conveying his wisdom to his son, however, requires that the father have recourse to the letters and the intelligence that is in the parable, and the father establishes the sublime wisdom via the letters and the understanding in the parable in which the wisdom is concealed. The letters of the parable and its thought nourish the child until he understands it with clarity, and afterward, if the child is wise, via the parable he will grasp something of the wisdom itself. According to this [analogy], the very letters of the parable resemble an irrigation pipeline through which flow the waters of a higher wisdom.[23]

In this way, the very concept of parable becomes a model of the divine strategy of *tzimtzum,* in which the infinite state of the Divine Wisdom—without effecting any change in itself—is reduced to a measure and form comprehensible to the human mind. Parable and *tzimtzum,* as understood by the Maggid, mirror one another and ultimately exemplify a single process.

In the parable, the infinite is scaled down to the level of finite comprehension and experience. Transcendent truth clothes itself in the parable, and as the entire cosmos is perceived to be a garment of the Divine, it follows implicitly that the whole cosmos, in a sense, is considered a kind of parable. Furthermore, as an accommodation of its sublime, infinite nature to this finite world and its plane of experience, the Torah itself in the particular, concrete, historical, and linguistic form as we know it is also a parable. Through the language and wording of the Torah—a product of *tzimtzum*—the spiritually perceptive person might be able to grasp something of the higher nature of the Torah transcending human language.[24]

While some considered parable dispensable once it had conveyed the wisdom contained in it, the Maggid's reference to the Torah as parable suggests an alternative model—the wisdom transmitted through the parable is never truly separable from the parable. The Maggid maintained that only through the Torah narratives, set in a finite reality governed by time, might one obtain a glimpse of the deeper nature of the Torah reflecting an infinite reality beyond time.[25]

For the Maggid, parable attempts to communicate what otherwise defies communication. And given the limitations of our understanding and of language, all of our thoughts and formulations—and even the sacred text of the Torah—are of the nature of parable. The nature of parable illuminates the Maggid's essential grasp of existence itself.[26]

What This Collection Comprises

In the parables included in the first part of this anthology, Paradox and the Unexpected, the reader will immediately recognize the surprise element and the presence of paradox. Although these qualities are hardly unique to the hasidic parable, they are very prominent elements in the parables of the hasidic masters and in the art of the hasidic parable.

The second part, Redefinitions, deals with parables that redefine basic concepts or themes in Jewish religious life and thought. As has been suggested above, redefinition is basic to the structure and nature of the hasidic parable. This type of parable was employed by hasidic teachers in order to challenge listeners to entertain the possibility of a different way of thinking, to redefine some of their basic conceptions, and to forge a different kind of religious consciousness.

The third part, Deepening the Implications of Divine Oneness, is devoted to parables representing one particular example of redefinition. Monotheism should not be understood simply as the rejection of other gods, but as the awareness that there is nothing apart from God—that in an ultimate sense there is only God. In this mystic deepening of the monotheistic belief, the entire cosmos is understood as a reflection and garment of God as the Divine is clothed in the world of being. As Rabbi Shneur Zalman of Lyady wrote in his work *Tanya,* "All that a person can see, sky and earth and its fullness, are but the garments of the Divine, which manifest their inner spirit, the divine life force that infuses them."[27] Nothing can exist, not even a thought, not even the most undesirable thought or emotion, unless it contains the spiritual life force, which alone gives it being. These parables express the realization, repeated many times in early hasidic texts, that the presence of God fills all being, that "there is no place devoid of God."[28]

The fourth part, Echoes and Transformations of Older Motifs, traces two parable traditions within hasidic texts and the background of their respective motifs through earlier stages of Jewish and perhaps even pre-Israelite thought. Within the hasidic parable, motifs with roots in much earlier stages of religious consciousness were remolded to suggest new meanings expressive of the hasidic ethos.

Parables with a strong historical context—those relating to polemics or issues surrounding the earlier history of Hasidism—are collected in the fifth and final part, The Polemics of an Hour of History. Some of these have to do with changes that occurred within the hasidic world; some with views concerning the place of Jewish thought and teaching vis-à-vis a larger and challenging cultural world. Some parables concern Hasidism's differences with the surrounding Jewish world, while others can be understood in terms of conflicts within the orbit of Hasidism itself. Among this last group are parables concerning the role of the *tzaddik*—the holy man at the center of the hasidic community—and latent tensions relating to that role. The parables in this part of the book mirror Hasidism's view of itself within the sometimes tempestuous storms of the times.

The parables I've chosen to include in this collection come from the early hasidic texts—essentially from the period of classical Hasidism, although I have included just a few slightly later examples because I find them valuable for their subject matter. All of them were chosen for their literary value, or because they convey something about the teaching and history of early Hasidism. Some were selected because they speak most readily to the spiritual quest of contemporary man and woman, and to the contemporary Jew in particular.

Although it has an obvious literary focus, this collection, with its commentaries and notes, also reflects my belief that parables are a most appropriate and available portal through which the contemporary reader may enter into the world of hasidic thought and become aware of the profound spiritual richness of that world. ➣

1. See Moshe Idel, "Reification of Language in Jewish Mysticism," p. 56; and Zeev Gries, *Sefer, sofer, ve-sippur be-reshit ha-ḥasidut,* p. 64.
2. 1741–1804. See Benno Heinemann, *The Maggid of Dubno and His Parables.*
3. For example, *Sha'ar ha-melekh: al mo'ade ha-shanah* by Mordecai ben Shmuel of Vilkatsh; a collection of sermons on the holy days and festivals of the Jewish year, which includes some twenty parables.
4. See Aryeh Wineman, *Beyond Appearances.*
5. David Stern, *Parables in Midrash,* p. 9.
6. Ibid., p. 7.
7. Zohar 1:245b.
8. B. Shabbat 153a.
9. Rachel Elior, "Hasidism: Historical Continuity and Spiritual Change," p. 322.
10. Beatrice Silverman Weinreich, ed., *Yiddish Folktales,* p. 7.

11. *Likkutim yekarim* (1974), #158.

12. *Or torah* (1910), 6b, Va-era.

13. *Or Yitzhak* (1961), p. 111, Bo.

14. Ibid., Introduction, p. 5.

15. Note Edward P.J. Corbett, *Classical Rhetoric,* pp. 77, 104.

16. This section of the Introduction draws upon material that appeared in my article "On the Hasidic Parable" and is included here with permission from *Judaism,* vol. 45, no. 3 (Summer, 1996). Copyright 1996, American Jewish Congress.

17. "In all our Torah, both the written Torah and the oral tradition, there is nothing, not even a single letter which speaks of anything other than the service of God (the worship of God in its most comprehensive sense)." Meshullam Feibush Heller of Zbarazh, *Yosher divre emet* (1974), #24, 15b.

18. *Toledot Ya'akov Yosef* (1973), I, p. 379, Emor.

19. Ibid., II, p. 650, Re'eh.

20. *Kedushat Levi* (1993), p. 459, Avot/Va-ethannan.

21. For an introduction to this concept, see Gershom Scholem, *Major Trends in Jewish Mysticism,* pp. 260–264. While the concept of *tzimtzum* is generally associated with Rabbi Isaac Luria's reformulation of kabbalistic thought in the late sixteenth century, that same concept, given a somewhat different ambience, is found also in the writings of Rabbi Moshe Cordovero (*haRamak*) who preceded Luria (*ha'Ari*) as the preeminent kabbalistic thinker and teacher in sixteenth-century Safed. Note Berakha Zack's article, "Rabbi Moshe Cordovero's Doctrine of *Tzimtzum,*" pp. 207–237. In general, while Hasidism employed terminology from Lurianic Kabbalah, Cordovero's teachings may have had a much more essential influence upon Hasidism and are more in consonance with the actual tenor of hasidic thought.

22. See Rivka Schatz Uffenheimer, *Hasidism as Mysticism,* for a brilliantly insightful study of the Maggid and his school and, hence, of the ideational ethos of classical Hasidism.

23. *Maggid devarav le-Ya'akov,* #131, p. 226.

24. Ibid., #5, 56, 126.

25. Ibid., #126; *Likkutim yekarim,* #285.

26. For a fuller examination of the role of parable in the Maggid's worldview, see Wineman, "Parables and *Tsimtsum,*" pp. 293–300.

27. *Tanya,* pt. I, chap. 42.

28. The Aramaic expression echoes the statement in *Midrash Shemot rabbah* 2:5 explaining God's revealing Himself to Moses via a desert shrub as a way of conveying that "there is no place devoid of the Shekhinah, not even a [small desert] shrub."

The Hasidic Parable

PARADOX
AND THE
UNEXPECTED

Sadness in Finding
a Treasure

⌒

"I rejoice in Your words as one who finds great booty" (Ps. 119:162). Why does the verse liken God's words to great booty? A parable of a man who, walking along the way, comes upon an enormous treasure with coins too numerous to count, and he takes from the treasure a great deal of money, all that he is able to carry, and he is exceedingly joyful. But when ready to leave, he notes that he has to leave behind a vast portion of the treasure as he has no containers with which to carry the great wealth, and this brings him distress.

And that is as it says, "I rejoice in your words," in what I learned and acquired. But in the end, though I learned much Torah, I don't consider that to my credit, because I am aware of the extent of Torah knowledge that I still lack; aware that all that I succeeded in acquiring of Torah is merely as a drop from the sea—as [the case of] that person who finds a great treasure. *(Or torah)*[1]

The above parable is found in a collection of comments on verses from the Book of Psalms in the name of the Maggid, Dov Baer of Mezherich (d. 1772). It echoes, however, an association found in a much earlier source, *Mekhilta derabbi Yishma'el*, a tanna'itic legal midrash on the

Book of Exodus, which contains the following comment: "Booty signifies Torah, as it is said, 'I rejoice in Your words as one who finds great booty'" (Ps. 119:162).[2]

The parable itself directly counters the reaction that the reader (or listener) expects from the person who finds such a great treasure. He assumes a response of happiness and gladness, but the person in the parable instead feels a pronounced sadness. A highly ironic thrust is cast upon the mention of rejoicing in the verse from Psalms that is quoted. The parable as related by the Maggid, however, is still more complex because the two parts of the text—the *mashal* and the *nimshal* (the parable story and its given explanation and application)—each have their own very different connotations. The *mashal*, taken by itself, would convey something long known about human nature—that a person is never satisfied, certainly not with material possessions. "The eye is not satiated with riches" (Eccl. 4:8; note also Prov. 27:20). For many, that persistent inability to be content negates the very possibility of happiness. As the sage Ben Zoma taught in the Mishnah,[3] "Who is rich? That person who rejoices in his lot"—whatever his lot may be. The *mashal* itself has the tenor of a wisdom parable and may well have been an independent parable that acquired a very different kind of application in the Maggid's interpretation.

The *nimshal* contains a personal confession, a realization on the part of the speaker, of the extent of Torah that he does not know. A person of knowledge, it follows, should, like Socrates, be humble in the face of all that he does not know.

In the background of the rise of eighteenth-century Hasidism lies a contention voiced by several of the early hasidic teachers, and perhaps foremost by Rabbi Ya'akov Yosef of Polonnoye, a critique of the world of talmudic learning in the traditional academy, the yeshivah, and in the rabbinic world at large. Talmudic scholars and rabbis, it was charged, were using learning as a means of satisfying one's own ego, engaging in the study of Torah as one might engage in a chess tournament with the aim of triumphing over others. Rather than Torah serving as a cure for pride and self-centeredness, it became instead a channel to express the idolatrous quality of pride. While various types of criticism of prevalent types of Torah learning are present also in somewhat earlier Eastern European Jewish texts,[4] the above criticism comprises a recurrent note in

classical hasidic sources. That kind of harsh criticism of the world of talmudic learning was certainly a factor in provoking hostility on the part of
the rabbinate and of the more conventional Jewish religious community—hostility that culminated in acts of excommunication of the followers of Hasidism in the latter decades of the eighteenth century. The parable
related by the Maggid, who himself enjoyed a reputation of being an accomplished talmudic scholar, presents a countermotif to the pride that the
Hasidim of the time attributed to members of the learned class among Jews.

In this light, the reader might ask whether the containers (*kelim,* also
tools or vessels) mentioned in the parable have a special meaning.
Perhaps the Maggid is implying that members of the aristocracy of learning who turn only to cognitive tools, tools of the mind, were employing
the wrong kind of tools; that tools of a more inner and spiritual nature
are also necessary in order truly to acquire the treasure of Torah. To the
mind of the Maggid and his students, Torah is more than a body of
knowledge to be acquired; it is an instrument of spiritual purification and
transformation. And knowledge by itself can sometimes have effects in
the very opposite direction.

The verse from Psalms that opens the parable likens God's word to
great *booty,* while the parable speaks instead of a great *treasure.* The word
found in the verse from Psalms, *shelal* (booty), suggests that the spoils of
battle, though ethically questionable, are nevertheless a kind of reward
for battle, whereas the word *otzar* (treasure) completely avoids any con-
notation of reward—of something that the person has merited in some
way. Finding such an unexpected treasure evokes unexpected joy, a joy
however that, as in the *mashal,* quickly turns into distress.

While in both the *mashal* and the *nimshal* the person's emotional lack
outweighs his gain, the thrust is decidedly different for each part of the
parable. In the *mashal,* the person experiences distress, whereas in the
nimshal he experiences humility. Perhaps the Maggid's rendition of the
parable ultimately suggests an additional nuance identifying humility
itself as a treasure.

---

1. *Or torah* (1910), 46b, *Tehillim.*
2. *Mekhilta derabbi Yishma'el,* Yitro, sec. 9.
3. M. Avot 4:1.
4. Mendel Piekarz, *Bi-yeme tzemihat ha-hasidut,* pp. 305–320.

The Clown on the Day
of Judgment

~

A king had designated a particular day of judgment that he might scrutinize the deeds of his subjects, and he instituted for that day all the mechanisms and protocol of judgment. When the people of the land heard of the great and awesome judgment, trepidation and despair came over them, and they cried out hopelessly, "Woe to us because of the day of judgment and rebuke and in particular because of the wrathful countenance of the king toward us, for our guilt is great. We failed to execute his commands, and we rebelled against him. And who will be able to endure his wrath? Certainly our defenders will be powerless to speak on our behalf in the face of the king's wrath, and our accusers will prevail."

The subjects reason that first they must attempt to remove the wrath of the king. What do they do? They choose one very wise man, with the likes of a clown. And when he comes before the king he begins speaking words of parable and imagery, words of desire and joy and of praise of the king's great and exalted state, and he includes many humorous things, proceeding from one parable to another, from one glad thing to another, as though he himself were not among the king's subjects standing in judgment—until he succeeds not only in removing the king's anger but also in giving the king joy and delight. . . .

And when the accusers noted that the king, with joy and favor, had become reconciled with his subjects, they ceased speaking and fled the scene, while those who defended the people prevailed and determined the course of the judgment. *(Or torah)*[1]

Having set the stage for a situation of awe and fear, the parable story then appears to escape from that very situation as it takes on the effects of fantasy and hyperbole. It has a charming ending, even though the hearer cannot avoid feeling that it is told in a tongue-in-cheek manner. Just imagine such an occurrence in a courtroom!

But the real significance of the parable applies on the level of the *nimshal*—the explanation of the story offered in the text. The *nimshal* refers to the importance of reciting the Verses of Song[2] along with the reading of passages concerning the sacrifices (offered in a festive context) and the reading of praises and blessings preceding the *Amidah*[3] on the holy day of Rosh Hashanah, even though inclusion of such utterances might seem thoroughly out of context on such an occasion of judgment.

The parable is related within a homily of the Maggid on a biblical verse, Psalms 81:4, "Blow the horn on the new moon, on the full moon for our feast day." Certainly by virtue of its mention of the horn (shofar), the verse was interpreted as referring to Rosh Hashanah and is, in fact, recited in the liturgy of that day. The holy day of Rosh Hashanah falls on the very beginning of the lunar month (the new moon) and the Hebrew word *ba-keseh* in that verse has, in fact, been understood both as the new moon and as the time when the light of the moon is covered, hence just preceding its reappearance.[4] The first day of the seventh month acquired, over time, both the name Rosh Hashanah (beginning of the year) and the association of a time of judgment. The parable may be echoing the opening verse of that psalm, "Sing joyously to God . . . take up a song, sound

the timbrel, the melodious lyre, and harp" (Ps. 81:1). The homilist, however, mentions the concluding word of the verse he is interpreting, *hagenu*
(feast day, festive day), and dissects the word *hag* (feast day) into its two
constituent letters, which he then interprets as suggestive of two of the
kabbalistic *sefirot* (forms and manifestations of the Infinite Divine Being
and Energy): *hesed* (lovingkindness) and *gevurah* (judgment). On the day
the shofar is sounded, judgment is transformed into lovingkindness. The
very demeanor of the king who judges is transformed from anger to kind-
ness.

The text of the parable includes also an interpretation of *zemirot*
(songs) that relates the root *zmr* (to sing) to another verb form with the
same root letters meaning to prune, as the song prunes the *kelipot* (the
demonic shells of the abyss), which, in Lurianic Kabbalah, comprise the
antithesis of the holy. Underlying this complicated network of reasoning
is the idea that joy can be a path of inner purification and atonement.

Comparing man's judgment before God in this parable to a more modern frame of reference, such as Kafka's *The Trial*,[5] the reader will note in
the hasidic parable a decidedly redeeming aspect in its conception of
judgment. The legal authority—the judge and the prosecution—evokes
deep anxiety and trembling, which then give way to a decisive lightening
of mood that flows from the unstated realization that, after all is considered, a child is standing in judgment before his or her own parent! The
clown figure is able to accomplish what serious pleading might be wholly
unable to effect, namely an annulment of the king's wrath. And this is
possible because, in the final analysis, the king's anger—as voiced in
many parables, especially those told by the Maggid's student, Rabbi Levi
Yitzhak of Berdichev—is itself but a mask disguising his love and compassion for his children. Beneath the veneer of the cruelty of judgment
lies another reality—that of redemptive joy.

The parable tends to reassess the function of poetry in the liturgy of a
season of judgment. The liturgical poems *(piyyutim)* serve not as an
expression of pleading, but rather as a way of providing delight to God.
The reader can detect in this parable a subtle nuance negating, from
within, the very scene of judgment.

As related by the Maggid, this parable extols the virtues of humor, of
song and poetry, and of the intrinsic joy felt in parable itself.

1. *Or torah,* on Psalms 81:4, 45a.
2. *Pesuke dezimra,* a section of the traditional morning prayers drawn largely from the Book of Psalms.
3. Considered the essential expression of prayer itself, the *Amidah* is recited silently while standing.
4. See B. Beitzah 16a.
5. London: Victor Gollancz, 1935.

Chipping Away
at the Mountain

༄

A king commanded his servants to raise up a very large mountain, removing it from its place—an impossible task. So his servants decided among themselves to dig and break up [shbr] the mountain into tiny pieces, so that each person would be able to carry a small portion appropriate to his own particular strength. And in this way they carried out the king's command.

Similarly in this way, God, the King of the universe, commands us to raise up the Holy Sparks. And it was for this very purpose that the *shevirah* [Breaking of the Vessels] came about: so that each person might then be able to raise up the fallen sparks, each one according to his own spiritual level. . . . (*Or torah*)[1]

The above parable, told by the Maggid, Dov Baer of Mezherich, begins with what would seem to be an utterly ludicrous and impossible command given by the king. However, using their intelligence, the servants find a way to execute it. Both the directive to move the large mountain from its place and the servants' strategy of breaking up the mountain into manageable parts—small pieces of rock and earth capable of being lifted and carried—would seem initially to be both unexpected and incomprehensible.

Then, in a feat of craftsmanship in the art of parable, the servants' strategy of breaking up (shbr) the mountain is connected, in the nimshal, with the shevirah (from the same root as shbr [to break up, shatter]—the primordial Shattering of the Vessels (shevirat ha-kelim), a significant concept in Lurianic Kabbalah. According to that teaching, a configuration of vessels bearing the Divine Light collapsed and was shattered, and some of the Holy Sparks fell into the abyss. Later they emerged, bringing evil into being. In its implied reference to this theme in Lurianic Kabbalah, the much more innocent action in the parable story acquires intense symbolic meaning.

Lifting up the Holy Sparks is part of the process of repairing and mending (tikkun) the entire cosmos, including the higher realms, the world of the Divine. According to Lurianic Kabbalah, the task of repairing the shattered vessels is given to humankind, and to the people of Israel in particular.[2] And in fact, that task accounts for human existence. The mending or repair of the cosmos, the repair of all the worlds, would seem to be an impossible task, far beyond anyone's capability, even beyond the collective capability of all humanity. The parable conveys, however, that each person is commanded to mend what he or she is capable of repairing in life, and the supreme task, like the moving of the mountain, is thus broken down to manageable and individual proportions. Not every person is capable of the same efforts with regard to tikkun; rather, each individual is expected to engage in the act of mending according to one's own individual capability.

Furthermore, the Maggid notes in his explanation that the Shattering of the Vessels actually occurred for the purpose of providing an opportunity for human beings to perform acts of tikkun—not the other way around as one might assume. Thus, while employing a key term from the teaching of Isaac Luria (1534–1572), the Maggid completely transformed the earlier conception of the Shattering of the Vessels, removing the sting of catastrophe from the concept. While in Lurianic Kabbalah, shevirat ha-kelim involved a primordial tragedy, the Maggid understood it instead as part of a divine strategy devised for the purpose of allowing each person to engage in the mending of his own existence and, through that effort, of existence itself. And so, while in the mashal, the king's servants break up the mountain, in the *nimshal,* it is God, presumably, who shatters the vessels as a purposeful and intentional act.

The biblical verse that occasions the parable and the homily is Psalm 126:1, which begins, "When the Lord restores the fortunes of Zion. . . ." The verb *shuv* (restore) suggested to the Maggid the restoration of God's name, a nullification of that shattering of the Divine Light and its vessels, a restored wholeness to the Divine and to all existence. In various kabbalistic and hasidic sources, these Holy Sparks are considered to infuse all of creation, and the Jew's specific role in *tikkun* consists of finding and redeeming those sparks, which are found in all of life. The material, physical world contains such concealed sparks, which man can discover when he elicits paths of spirituality precisely within what is physical in nature. Fulfilling a mitzvah with devotion and proper intent redeems the sparks that are concealed within all the aspects and activities of life.

In his homily, the Maggid explained one aspect of the process by which man is able to raise those fallen sparks, the Holy Letters, divine in nature, which came to permeate all being. In the psychology of the Maggid, those letters come to a person in the form of thoughts that are in need of repair. They may be thoughts exemplifying lower or fallen forms of love or fear or glory or triumph—all thoughts that contain a holy core but that must be purified and elevated to the level of the hidden Holy Spark that they contain. Such thoughts can sometimes evoke a distinct sense of shame in a person that draws the person to humility, even to the point of negating a sense of his very existence. And precisely in that state he is able to sense the very highest realms of being, the highest of the *sefirot,* speaking through his own thoughts, even through those thoughts that come to him in distasteful form.

Many of the parable motifs circulated throughout the hasidic world are heard in parables told by various masters. The following parable, clearly related to the above, was told by Rabbi Nahman of Bratslav (1772–1810), who was born in the same year as the Maggid's death.

A parable of a king who sent his son to a distant place that there he might learn various types of wisdom [the sciences]. Afterward the son returned to his father's house learned in all the different sciences as was fitting for him. Once the king commanded the son to lift a certain very large stone, such as a millstone [used in grinding wheat] and carry it up to the attic of his house. Now of course the son would not be able to raise the stone due to its huge size and weight, and the son was distressed that it was not possible for him to carry out his father's will, until the king later disclosed his thinking and explained to him, "Do you really think that I would order you to take such a heavy stone and actually lift it up? Would you be able to do such a thing, even with your great knowledge? Certainly that was not my intent at all. Rather, my intent was that you take a strong hammer and strike and shatter the stone into small pieces that you could then proceed to carry up to the attic." *(Shivḥe Moharan)*[3]

Rabbi Nahman then explained his parable in this way:

In this manner, God commands us to elevate our hearts to God on high, but our hearts are hearts of stone—heavy stone—such that it is completely impossible for one to raise it to God unless he take a hammer and break and shatter the heart of stone; then he would be able to lift it. And the actual hammer consists of our speech.[4]

With an allegorical explication quite different from that of the rather similar parable told earlier by the Maggid, Rabbi Nahman of Bratslav was alluding to the distinction found in Ezekiel 36:26: "And I will give you a new heart and put a new spirit into you: I will remove the heart of stone from your body and give you a heart of flesh." The Bratslaver explained the shattering of the stone as a change within a person, his conquering and annulling of his own stubbornness or of his own seeming inability to respond. Shattering his own heart of stone allows for an awakening of the heart—an "elevated" heart.

In Rabbi Nahman's parable, the spoken word assumes the role of a hammer striking a heavy stone. The word, which is weightless when compared with the heavy stone, becomes the tool for accomplishing the task expected of the powerful hammer! This parable of Rabbi Nahman of Bratslav conveys the idea that the spoken word, associated with both the reciting of psalms and the personal prayers of contrition uttered in a state of solitude, can affect the human heart, which is itself often characterized as resistant and made of stone.[5]

1. *Or torah* on Psalms 126:1, 47a. The same basic parable and discussion are also found in *Maggid devarav le-Ya'akov* (1976), #173.
2. In an age of religious persecution and hostility when the followers of different religious traditions perceived one another as foreign and threatening—even as representing the demonic—kabbalistic and hasidic thought generally refers to the human role and task in terms of the Jew alone.
3. *Shivhe Moharan,* "Ma'alat ha-hitbodedut," #5. (1962), 23ab.
4. Ibid.
5. See the version of the same parable in the collection of Rabbi Nahman's teachings, *Sefer hishtapkhut ha-nefesh,* #48, p. 23b. Note also *Likkute etzot,* "Hitbodedut," #16.

God in Transit

~

ere is a sweet parable that I heard spoken by our master, our rabbi and teacher, the Maggid of the holy congregation of Ravini,[1] that though we are in bitter exile, as is evident now, there are people able to attain holy inspiration [ru'ah ha-kodesh] more easily than was the case in the days of the Prophets. For in that earlier time one needed oaths and intense solitude, as is known, in order to attain prophecy and divine inspiration.

And [the Maggid] told a wondrous and sweet parable, that when a king is at home in his palace—in the place of his glory—should a friend of the king come and wish to invite the king to his home for a meal, the king would no doubt be angry with that person, for it is not considered proper for a king to leave his palace to go to another's home, even for a meal of exceptional quality, and it would never occur that one would invite the king to his home without first making all the preparations and inviting outstanding speakers so that the king should desire to attend his meal.

But when the king is journeying on the road and wishes to find a place to stay overnight, when he finds a clean place in a clean inn, even if it be in a village, just so that it is clean, he will stay overnight in that place.

And the *nimshal* is perfectly clear: At the time when the Temple stood and God's holy presence was in the House of the Holy of Holies, then it required tremendous effort for a person to receive [draw from God] holy inspiration or prophecy. . . .[2] But now, in the bitterness of exile, the holy Shekhinah[3] is in exile together with us and, because of our many iniquities, She wanders throughout the world and greatly desires to find a lodging in which to dwell, a clean place in which to rest. She seeks a person who is simply pure of transgressions and sins. Then that person becomes Her dwelling and She finds grace in the words of a wise person. *(No'am Elimelekh)*[4]

The above parable, which Rabbi Elimelekh of Lyzhansk had heard from the Maggid, is included in his interpretation of the names of the sons of the biblical patriarch, Jacob. The name Zebulun (one of Jacob's sons) suggests the noun *zvul*, which signifies a residence, in particular the Temple that once stood in Jerusalem. Elimelekh saw in that association the intent of the Shekhinah (the Divine Presence) to find a dwelling place during the exile when the Temple was no longer standing. While the exegetical context, in this case, appears forced and unconvincing, the thought in the parable is quite transparent.

With a slightly different emphasis, the same basic motif and theme are present also in the following parable related by Moshe Hayyim Efrayim of Sedilikov:

A stranger who journeys to a strange place where he has no friends normally has no one to whom he can relate what has happened to him, no one with whom to share what is in his heart. But when he meets a fellow stranger he feels free to befriend him, and each tells the other all that has happened to him.

God is like a stranger in this world, having no one over whom He may cast His presence. As Israel is also a stranger in this world, God therefore will not conceal from Israel His mitzvot.[5] *(Degel maḥane Efrayim)* [6]

In another version of the parable in the same text, recalling Abraham's status as a resident alien in the land of Canaan (Genesis 23:4), Efrayim of Sedilikov added in the *nimshal,* "The Patriarchs lived as strangers in this world, and the two strangers, God and the Patriarch . . . befriended one another" *(Degel maḥane Efrayim).*[7]

Without ignoring the social, historical, and geographical alienation involved in living in exile *(galut),* these parables nevertheless negate any sense that the Jew in exile is necessarily living in a state of alienation from God. On the contrary, the above parables view God as more accessible to the person who shares the transit status and the alienation that God also experiences as the Divine is rejected and considered a stranger in the world. Whether as an indirect response to the messianic awakening centered around Shabbetai Zevi[8] and its ensuing crisis or to Hasidism's innate sense of spiritual fulfillment in the present, spiritual redemption, it was felt, could occur even during exile. The Jew's historical situation did not preoccupy the Hasid; nor did it cause him to alter his historical reality in any practical way. The opportunity for a spiritual bonding with God, it was felt, is ever present and hence exists even in exile, especially in exile, because it provides greater opportunities for God to relate to man and befriend him and to allow man to experience union with the Divine.

The reader may observe the Hasid's response to exile and its tribulations, namely his refusal to react negatively to his situation and to totally subject his inner self to the fact and impact of living in exile. The parable is a subtle but emphatic transvaluation that places the state of exile, with all its limitations, on a level higher than the earlier state of national independence with the active functioning of the Temple in Jerusalem.

Comparing the Holy One, blessed be He, to a homeless traveler, a fellow stranger, displays a striking freshness and, in a single stroke, shatters

all accepted and conventional images of the Divine. The parable brings
God down to human dimensions and kindles in the listener a strong feeling of empathy with God. The image of the Divine provided in the parable is neither that of a cosmic king nor of the Infinite, but rather that of
a traveler bearing all the pain of being a stranger and (in the parable
related by Efrayim of Sedilikov) even an outcast. Such a parable reveals
an utterly unconventional dimension in the hasidic mind.

The parable reflects the earlier conceptions of the Exile of the
Shekhinah. These include the rabbinic concept of the Divine Presence
accompanying Israel in exile after the destruction of the Temple, formerly
its dwelling place in the world; and also the kabbalistic rereading of that
much earlier rabbinic concept as a condition of suffering, disharmony,
and displacement experienced by the Divine who is exiled from himself
and subjugated to evil powers. Israel's experience of exile on a historical
plane was thought to reflect that Divine experience of a greater Exile, a
deeper displacement and alienation on a cosmic kabbalistic plane.

The unusual image of God as a traveler in need had the power to speak
to the hearts of those Jews in Eastern Europe for whom the brunt of displacement and exile were basic and tragic facts of their reality, facts however that Jews could also transcend through a sense of the presence and
nearness of God even in exile.

---

1. Referring to the Maggid of Mezherich, who formerly served as a *maggid* in Rovno
   (Rovini).
2. Mention is made here of the joyous ceremony of the Drawing of the Water (*simḥat beit
   ha-sho'evah*). During the Second Temple period, this ceremony took place during the
   festival of Sukkot, which the homilist understood as an opportune and accessible time
   to draw prophecy and holy inspiration.
3. The Divine Presence, which, in the tradition of Kabbalah, became identified with
   malkhut, the lowest of the *sefirot;* the basically feminine *sefirah,* which suffers the pain
   of exile and separation from the higher manifestations of the Godhead, especially from
   the masculine *tiferet.*
4. *No'am Elimelekh* (1992), p. 83, Va-yeshev. Rabbi Shneur Zalman of Lyady (in the
   Tanya—Likkute amarim, chap. 33) echoes this parable motif when he speaks of the joy
   of the commoner when the king avails himself of that person's hospitality and lodges
   beneath his roof.

5. Commandments, holy deeds. The reader notes a subtle disparity rather than equivalence in the terms of the parable: while the human king tells his troubles, pouring out his heart to a fellow stranger, God instead remains on a higher plane and discloses His mitzvot.

6. *Degel maḥane Efrayim* (1963), p. 183, Be-har.

7. Ibid., p. 54, Va-yeshev.

8. The messianic movement that arose in the mid-seventeenth century and which, after attracting a wide following in many geographical areas, provoked a deep crisis in Jewry when the messianic figure himself converted to Islam in order to avoid execution.

The Correct Motivation

〜

parable told about two brothers, one of whom was wealthy, the other poor. The poor brother asked his rich brother, "What accounts for your wealth?" and he answered him, "It is because I do evil deeds." The poor brother then went and forsook the Lord and did as his brother, but his evil actions bore no fruit. He returned to inquire, "See, I have done as you do, and why hasn't success come my way?" This time the rich brother answered him, "It is because you have done evil only in expectation of wealth and not for the sake of the evil deeds themselves." *(Degel maḥane Efrayim)*[1]

This parable, related by both Efrayim of Sedilikov and Ya'akov Yosef of Polonnoye, startles the reader as the *kavvanah* (the inner intent and devotion) of a sinner is held up as a model! Even evil—the parable conveys with tongue in cheek—one must do with a wholeness of motivation! It is this very negative image of inner devotion and commitment that makes the parable so striking. The parable implicitly conveys the converse—that in serving God and in following a path of holiness, one's deeds must be done selflessly for the sake of God rather than in pursuit or expectation of any personal reward, even that of self-satisfaction. The reader understands that the parable can easily be stated in another version in which the poor brother turns to the path of good deeds but without the proper motivation.

In a section of his legal code, Maimonides defined the clear distinction between *avodah mi-yirah* (serving God out of fear) and *avodah me-ahavah* (serving God out of love).[2] In the former, one seeks to serve God and follow the Torah with an eye toward avoiding punishment and obtaining reward, whereas in the latter one seeks to do the same without any consideration of reward or punishment. The consequence of one's action relating to the person himself is irrelevant to the importance of doing the deed. One should strive to engage in divine service (*avodah*) and the life of Torah for its own sake without regard for reward. The tenor of this distinction, stated with such clarity by Maimonides, is carried over with even greater emphasis in hasidic teaching, which so often conveys that a concern for self impugns one's otherwise positive and holy act. Efrayim of Sedilikov taught that one's motivation in prayer should be the healing of the Shekhinah and hence the restoration of the true Oneness of God rather than the fulfillment of one's own personal needs. This thought is further connected with the Maggid's conception of the prayer experience as a transcendence of the self, even a total forgetting of the self; concern for one's own needs or desires is therefore inconsistent with the very nature of prayer.

Efrayim of Sedilikov's homily, which includes this parable, relates to the concluding portion (Be-ḥukkotai) of Leviticus (26:3–27:34). The first part of that Torah portion focuses directly upon reward and punishment, blessings and curses. It begins: "If you follow My laws and faithfully observe My commandments, I will grant you rains in their season. . . ." Efrayim of Sedilikov's reading of that same portion subtly negates all concern for reward and punishment, as these are incompatible with a purity of motivation. As is conveyed in numerous hasidic parables and homilies that focus so strongly upon the intent and mindset with which a deed is performed, an impure motivation negates the very character of a holy act and makes of it a way of serving the self rather than of serving God.

Within classical hasidic teaching, the implications of the above parable relate to every kind of mitzvah, and to prayer and Torah study in particular. The word *mitzvah* itself was explained by the Maggid not as "commandment" (from the verb root *tzava*) but rather from the word *tzavta*, meaning "together," an act in which both man and God are present together.[3] This conception of mitzvah would necessarily require the proper intent and motivation and a person's complete presence in the act. Hasidic teaching emphasizes even more forcefully that prayer requires the correct motivation and intent. And hasidic homilies of this period reiterate the charge that the study of Torah, though a sacred pursuit, is grossly distorted when a student or a scholar engages in Torah with the wrong motives. A great deal of criticism was directed to the world of the talmudic academies and toward the rabbinate for employing study and erudition in the service of pride, sometimes to the point of utilizing one's knowledge to embarrass and vanquish others. In a text containing the teachings of the Maggid of Mezherich, a passage asserts that Beit Shammai, the students of the famous sage in early talmudic times, exhibited greater sharpness in their learning than did Beit Hillel, the students of the rival sage, Hillel. The views of Beit Hillel, however, came to be favored in the consequent crystallization of talmudic law, for the value of devotion exceeds that of intellectual prowess (lamdanut).[4] And just as in prayer it is crucial to "know before Whom you stand" (words often inscribed on the ark containing the Torah scrolls in the synagogue), so it is necessary for a student to know "before Whom one studies."[5] It is possible to do the right thing even with the wrong motivation.

---

1. *Degel mahane Efrayim* (1963), pp. 186–187, Be-ḥukkotai; also found in *Toledot Ya'akov Yosef* (1973), p. 30, Bereshit.
2. *Mishneh Torah, Hilkhot teshuvah,* chap. 10.
3. *Likkutim yekarim* (1974), #136.
4. Ibid., #124.
5. Ibid., #59.

The Talking Bird

~

A parable of a king of flesh and blood who has a bird that talks. The king entertains himself with that bird and looks after it, and he turns from his own exalted level of intelligence in order to listen to the bird. He finds greater joy and delight in this bird than in all the intelligent discourse of his officials because the talking bird is a highly unusual phenomenon. *(Likkutim yekarim)*[1]

The opening of the above parable conveys the impression of a king who squanders his time and interest with an entertaining bird. In the art of this particular parable, such a foolish king, however, comes to represent God.

This parable of the talking bird, presumably related here by the Maggid, Dov Baer of Mezherich, and alluded to in other homilies of the Maggid,[2] is found also in a homily of Rabbi Levi Yitzhak of Berdichev, who commented on the parable passage as follows:

> If so, then you, human beings, open your eyes and realize the greatness of the level of mitzvot and good deeds, for all the worship offered by the angels on high is considered as nothing in comparison with human deeds. . . . *(Kedushat Levi)*[3]

The parable elicits the question, "Why is the spectacle of the speaking bird such a wonder that people would travel a great distance just to see it?" After all, humans are also capable of speaking! The difference between the human and the talking bird, though obvious enough, is explained: it is understood that humans are capable of speaking, but a talking bird is quite unusual. Similarly, as Rabbi Levi Yitzhak of Berdichev explains in the *nimshal,* it is expected that the hosts of angels worship and praise God, for such worship is deemed natural for them. For the human being, however, worship is not really a natural and expected act, and in this respect human worship of God can be likened to the speech of a bird. Furthermore, given the human makeup and man's distractions, given his concern with the material and his evil propensities, and given also the human capacity of choice, it is really unnatural for man to engage in the worship and service of the Divine. And precisely for these reasons, God values worship on the part of humans above worship by the angels. Like the talking bird, the unnaturalness of human worship makes it something rare and precious.

Why is it important and necessary that man's turning to the service of God be, by nature, so unusual? The passage cited above from *Likkutim yekarim* poses the following question: "Why did the Holy One, blessed be He, place the human soul in a mortal, material body and situate him in this lower, material realm of being?" Given the claim that the soul is divine in origin and nature, this question, raised already in the Zohar,[4] is of real significance. Could not God have created man like the angels?

The Maggid answers his own question by referring to the delight that God receives from the *tzaddik* (the holy man). It is imperative in the overall scheme of things that God's created beings serve Him precisely from within this imperfect material world—a world that does not impel or even encourage man to follow a spiritual path, and a world in which the Divine, though ever present, is also concealed. According to the hasidic worldview, the sage emphasized that the totality of being in all its realms is inseparable from God, the holy life source of all existence, and nevertheless it is crucial that the Divine—the good and the holy—also give rise to a material world. This is necessary because only from within such a physical reality with its propensity toward evil can the holy, the Divine, truly realize itself on a cosmic level. As the Maggid explains elsewhere, the task of the *tzaddik* is to transform the likes of concrete, corporeal being (yesh) into ayin,[5] the Divine, which underlies and transcends all being, and that kind of transformation can take place only from within a world of yesh. Material reality conceals the Divine, and in a host of parables the Maggid stressed that only in such a world in which God's Presence is concealed is it possible to seek the Divine Presence. Only in this kind of world is it possible to transform evil into good, to transform the earthly into what is holy, as man seeks God's Presence even where that Presence is hidden. As Rabbi Shneur Zalman of Lyady (a student of the Maggid) wrote in the Tanya, "There is no joy before God comparable with the light and joy of that light which emerges from within the darkness itself."[6]

The Maggid adds that although the human being erroneously considers himself a lowly creature incapable of bringing delight to God, the latter "turns from the song of all the infinity of worlds, and all the angels hasten to hear the words of man."[7] Possessing a body that is subject to frailty and lust, man tends to think of himself as, by nature, remote from any potential for a true relationship with God. Hasidism inherited from various streams of medieval thought an often negative estimation of the body, and in light of that viewpoint, it is striking that in the Maggid's creative reading of a talmudic saying referring to the "house of God,"[8] it is the physical body, potentially so weak and crude with desires that can lead man to sin, that is viewed as the (ideal) dwelling place of God.[9]

The parable of the talking bird and its explanation convey the utter rarity and the consequent preciousness of spirituality on the part of a human being.

---

1. Likkutim yekarim (1974), #220.
2. For example, in Or ha-emet (1960), 2b.
3. Kedushat Levi ha-shalem (1993), p. 194, Tazria.
4. Zohar 1:245a.
5. Maggid devarav le-Ya'akov (1976), #190.
6. Tanya, Likkute amarim, chap. 33.
7. Op. cit., Or ha-emet.
8. B. Berakhot 3a.
9. Op. cit., Or ha-emet.

Compassion as Punishment

king whose minister rebelled against him wishes to take revenge against his minister in such a way that the minister will regret what he had done. What does the king do? He elevates the minister to a higher rank, and consequently the minister is very embarrassed and hence unable to act rebelliously against the king. And this sense of shame is more difficult for him than all the punishments in the world, for he is constantly distressed at what he had done, and he thinks, "How can I lift up my head knowing that I have rebelled against such a great king who is gracious and forgiving at the expense of his own honor and who promoted me to an even higher position than I previously had?" And as a result of his shame and distress, he takes his own life out of respect for the king, for he has come to prefer death to life. *(Divre Menaḥem)*[1]

The above parable, found in a homily by Menahem Mendel of Rymanov—a student of Elimelekh of Lyzhansk who led a hasidic community in Rymanov in southeastern Poland until his death in 1815—shares with any number of hasidic tales the pattern of a person doing something seemingly bizarre and irrational, which upon explanation is seen to possess a definite logic. In the parable story, any other punishment would have caused the minister to regret his rebellion because of the consequences incurred rather than to regret his act of rebellion itself.

This parable is included in Menahem Mendel's exegetical exercise attempting to resolve the question, "How is it possible that after experiencing the Divine Glory at the scene of the Revelation at Sinai, the Israelites could respond by requesting that they themselves not hear the Divine Utterances (Exod. 20:16)?" The preacher uses the parable to explain that the Israelites, standing at Sinai and witnessing the wondrous Revelation, were utterly ashamed of their deeds and feared that their deeds warranted their death. Menahem Mendel of Rymanov quoted a statement attributed to the Baal Shem Tov on the nature of divine revenge: When God wishes to take revenge against the Israelites, He actually gives light to them with all the beneficial effects of the divine plenitude (shefa). For when that occurs, they feel their shame and experience regret for their iniquities as they ask themselves the question similar to that asked by the king's minister in the parable, "How is it that we transgressed the will of such a great and awesome King who is so good and compassionate to us?" The parable comes to exemplify the paradoxical nature of that rather strange form of divine revenge.

With its fiercely surprising turn along with its humorous dimension, the parable reveals an insightful grasp of human nature and response, but one that (the reader suspects) might not take into consideration an utterly shameless person!

Another version of the same parable story is found in *Toledot Ya'akov Yosef*, Bo.[2] There a villager rebels against the king and does such things as striking and throwing stones at the icons of the king. The king first responds by giving the rebel a position of leadership and then continues to elevate him until he becomes second only to the king. In the process, the villager witnesses the glory of the king and his court and the king's merciful ways, and he becomes more and more distressed that he had rebelled against such a king. The king intentionally brings him to a high position in his court, for if he were to put him to death the rebel would know only a temporary distress, whereas now he experiences ongoing and unceasing shame. As in the version told by the Rymanover, the parable found in *Toledot* similarly bears out the paradox that being an object of compassion deepens one's sense of guilt and distress.

In both versions of the parable, the homiletic context attributes to the Baal Shem Tov an interpretation of Psalms 94:1, "God of retribution, Lord, God of retribution, appear!" Divine revenge consists of compassion, which can actually comprise the greatest pain. Taking off on a Torah reference to eating the *pesah* (the roasted animal whose blood was sprinkled on the doorposts of the Israelites' dwellings), together with both unleavened bread and bitter herbs (Exod. 12:8), Rabbi Ya'akov Yosef goes on to explain a question raised in another Torah verse, "When all these things befall you—the blessing and the curse—and you take them to heart amidst the various nations to which the Lord your God has banished you and you then return to God . . . sincerely and wholeheartedly . . ." (Deut. 30:1–2).[3] It is understood that afflictions and the working out of a curse might bring one to turn toward God *(teshuvah)*, but how can a blessing and good fortune accomplish the same end? Utilizing the parable as a model, Rabbi Ya'akov Yosef explains that such good fortune and compassion can evoke the profoundest sense of shame, which in turn can direct a person to turn to God.

The parable as told by Menahem Mendel of Rymanov adds a concluding narrative motif, one which does not appear in the earlier text, namely the rebel's taking of his own life out of his deep shame. This conclusion of the *mashal* might be understood as a parallel to the Israelites' fear that they might die in the wake of their experiencing the awesome Divine Presence at the hour of Revelation.[4]

---

1. *Divre Menahem* (1935), pp. 13–14, Va-ethannan.

2. *Toledot Ya'akov Yosef* (1973), I, pp. 166–167, Bo.

3. It is reported that a parable of this type was told by the Baal Shem Tov himself in reference to Deuteronomy 30:1 according to Ya'akov Kapel of Kosov, *Ahavat shalom;* see Shimon Menahem Mendel of Gavartchov, *Baal Shem Tov al ha-torah* (Jerusalem) II, p. 230, n.d.

4. Exodus 20:16.

That Each Occasion Be like the Very First

⌒

A lovely parable ascribed to the Besht [the Baal Shem Tov]. A king had in his employ a man who excelled at playing the violin, a person who, in his playing, attained the far reaches of beauty, and the king especially loved one particular melody that he played. The king would command the musician to perform that melody for him in his palace every day, even several times a day. And the musician would do exactly as the king requested.

But after a while the melody grew old and stale in the eyes of the musician who no longer found the same desire and awakening in playing the melody as he once did. What did the king do to restore to the musician an inner awakening of desire and love for that melody? Each time he wished to hear that melody in which he so delighted, the king would call in a new person whom he found in the marketplace, one who had never before heard that melody. That person was hearing it for the very first time, and the musician's playing of the melody in his presence restored vitality and enthusiasm to his performance. The king continued in that practice over a long period of time.

Sometime later, the king took counsel concerning what else he might do with the musician because it was troublesome for the king each time to have to invite a new person from the marketplace in order to rekindle enthusiasm in the musician. And the king was advised to blind the eyes of the musician so that the latter would never again be able to discern the image of a person. And every time the king desired to hear that melody he would simply inform the musician, "Behold a new man has now come who has never heard your melody," and renewed delight would be kindled in the musician. For having no eyes to discern the figure of a person, he really believed that new persons were constantly coming [who had never before heard the melody]. *(Or ha-me'ir)*[1]

In his homily, Ze'ev Wolff of Zhitomir related the above parable to the Jew's reciting formulary prayers before God, with the danger that with repetition, the act of prayer, like the violinist's melody, can become stale and lose its inner vitality. The parable is one expression of an ongoing and deep-rooted tension in Jewish worship between *keva* and *kavvanah*, between accepted form, structure, and expression on one hand and spontaneity in prayer on the other.

Recognizing this tension, Ze'ev Wolff of Zhitomir asserted that each act of prayer has its own experiential context according to each person's unique experience at that particular moment, and the uniqueness of the present moment enables a person to pray as though he had never prayed those words before. They become, in effect, as new words.

While the story's jarring conclusion might perhaps belong to an older, independent tale, the parable with its explication insists that the familiar words of prayer must always be experienced as new; that the familiar must be experienced as something emphatically unfamiliar. Contrary to the wording of the parable text, the reader intuitively grasps that the task of perpetual renewal falls not upon the King (God), but rather upon the worshiper. Just as in the parable, in order to retain the melody's inner power it is the musician who must always feel that he is playing that melody for the very first time, so the person praying must relate to the words of prayer as though he is reciting them for the very first time. While repetition can prove to be deadening, Hasidism also presumed that the tradition of prayer, which it accepted as part of normal Jewish practice and law, contains the ability for the worshiper to discover, each time, new life and fresh meaning in the familiar words.

As Menahem Mendel of Rymanov commented on the same subject:

> Anyone with a brain in his head can realize that even in the presence of a human king of flesh and blood, it is neither respectful nor proper to stand and recite to him each day the same identical song without adding something new or different. And all the more so is it the case [when one stands] before the King, the Holy One, blessed be He, who knows one's heart and inward parts; in His presence it is necessary to renew the inner devotion of the heart continually each day, as it is written, "Sing to the Lord a *new* song" (Ps. 149:1). *(Divre Menaḥem)* [2]

Still later, Rabbi Menahem Mendel of Kotsk is said to have pronounced the following judgment: "The person who prays because he prayed yesterday—a totally wicked person is better than him!"[3]

In the above parable ascribed to the Besht, one can recognize the analogy between prayer *(tefillah)* and song. Each true performance of a song must be a fresh and new event in its own right, not a repetitive act. The singer must be fully involved in every rendition of the song in order for it to become a new song.

Ze'ev Wolff explained the conclusion of the parable as an indication of God's preference that the worshiper's eyes be closed to this world with its temporal order so that he might envision instead that higher realm which is above time and hence above the danger of repetition. While this would seem to be a rather forced interpretation of the story's conclusion, it is interesting to note Ze'ev Wolff's conception of the higher realm of being as one that transcends time—a realm in which the very problem addressed in the story would not exist; where a perpetual state of inner awe and awakening could never succumb to the deadening effects of repetition. Ze'ev Wolff describes that higher realm as one in which a moment—like an experience—would never grow old, and each moment and each act, each song and prayer, would tirelessly glow with the fullness and depth and power of its own inwardness.

Ze'ev Wolff of Zhitomir explained this interpretation as the inner meaning of the text of *Kohelet* (Ecclesiastes), which seemingly reflects an experiencing of the world as ceaselessly repetitive.

The same essential issue, relating to the words of Torah—and in particular to the passages of the *Shema*[4] that are continually read and recited—goes back to a classical rabbinic text, the *Sifre,* in its comment on Deuteronomy 6:6, "'Take to heart these words which I charge you *this day*'—You should not think of these words as an old edict of the king, one already familiar to you; rather you must regard it as a new pronouncement which, therefore, all run to read."[5] You must relate to these words always, as something that is new, as a statement that is proclaimed today for the first time. Rabbi Levi Yitzhak of Berdichev defined the higher level of religious consciousness that a Jew might attain as analogous to the capacity to always see the words of the Torah as new.[6]

---

1. *Or ha-me'ir* (1995), II, pp. 331–332, *Kohelet.*
2. *Divre Menahem* (1935), p. 6, Be-shallah.
3. Martin Buber, *Or ha-ganuz,* p. 437, taken from *Nifla'ot hadashot.*
4. Three passages from the Torah that are recited daily in the morning and evening.
5. *Sifre* on Deuteronomy 6:6. *Sifre devei rav* (1864), 74a.
6. *Kedushat Levi ha-shalem* (1993), p. 264, Ki Tavo.

The Evil Inclination

~

T he Evil Inclination [*yetzer ha-ra*] can be likened to one who goes running among people, and his hand is closed shut, no one knowing what he is holding in it. And he deceives people and asks each person, "What am I holding in my hand?" To each person it seems as though he is holding whatever that particular person happens to desire. And so everyone runs after him thinking that whatever he desires is in that runner's hand. But afterwards, the person running opens his hand and it is empty.

Similarly, the Evil Inclination deceives the whole world; everyone pursues it as it deceives each and every person into thinking that whatever he desires is in its hand, each person according to his foolishness and his lusts and desires. And afterwards, in the end, it opens its hand and there is nothing in it, for no one can satisfy his desires through it.

Worldly desires can also be likened to rays of sunlight, which appear like pillars of light within a house. But if one grabs those pillars of light to hold them, he discovers that there is nothing at all in his hand. Such is the case with worldly desires. *(Siḥot Haran, #6)*[1]

The classical rabbinic view of humanity regards each person as having both a good and an evil inclination. Rabbi Nahman of Bratslav, a great-grandson of the Baal Shem Tov, here identifies the Evil Inclination with worldly desire and striving.

The above excerpt resembles a fusion of fable and allegory in its personification of the Evil Inclination as a figure in the story. The appeal of the Evil Inclination is its almost magical aspect, as individuals view it in terms of fulfilling their own personal desires. The surprising disappointment, however, is that it brings a sense of futility and vanity to life's strivings. But that same futility in the total context of the parable expresses not a nihilistic attitude but rather a moral and spiritual orientation to life.

Rabbi Nahman constructed the above parables employing the deception of appearances, a narrative tool that conveys the deception of desire itself. In this way the parables question some basic attitudes that people hold concerning striving and the pursuit of desire. In and of itself, desire is not only evil but also futile, for desire in the long run proves to be both insatiable and empty.

The above parable reflects the impulse toward paradox so central in both the thought and the stories of Rabbi Nahman of Bratslav.

---

1. Included in *Shivhe Haran*, p. 7.

REDEFINITIONS

The Crown and
the Container

great king made for himself a royal crown and prepared a container and frame in which to keep and conceal the crown so that it might remain in good condition. The shape of the container, it stands to reason, is also beautiful, and it has tiny openings through which the crown may be seen. When people come to the king's palace and see the container, the fool thinks, "How lovely is this vessel," for he lacks the wisdom to grasp that the real object of importance and value is not the container but rather what is inside—the crown. The internal is what is essential. The wise man, however, the person "with eyes in his head" (Eccl. 2:14) thinks, "Certainly the container is not the real feature," and he squints to gaze through the tiny holes until he catches a glimpse of the crown itself and experiences delight in it. *(Or Yitzhak)*[1]

The above parable is found in a text, *Or Yitzhak*, which was published only in 1961 from an old manuscript found among a collection of books passed down through the family of the author. Yitzhak of Radvil, who died in 1831, was in his earlier years a student of the Maggid, Dov Baer of Mezherich, as was his father, Michael Yehiel of Zlotshev,[2] an important hasidic figure in Eastern Galicia.[3] The reader of this parable realizes that the king does not intend to conceal the crown completely.

To the contrary, he intentionally prepares tiny openings in the exquisite container. However, those openings are so small that they require an effort on the part of the observer to perceive what is in the container. And this effort depends upon the person's understanding that the internal rather than the external is of primary significance, all else being secondary.

The image of the container in the parable suggests several different meanings. The vessel holding and concealing the crown might suggest the world itself in which the divine life force (ḥiyyut, "life quality and vitality"), though concealed, is present, giving life to all that is. The *yesh* (literally "that which is"; concrete, corporeal reality as known to sensory perception or investigation) itself exists only because there is clad in it the *ayin* (literally, "nothingness"), the divine reality that is beyond all that we deem "real" on the level of our sensory experience. The world—and the worlds—are but a garment of the Divine, who is present and concealed within the *yesh*. The parable recalls the saying of Rabbi Judah ha-Nasi in the Mishnah: "Do not look at the flask but rather at what it contains."[4] As the Maggid, Dov Baer of Mezherich, taught, "the essence of everything that is in the world is the spirituality within it, which comes from God [and is of God] who gives it existence."[5]

In light of the parable, one might add that while the *yesh* conceals that unseen spirituality that is the substratum of all being, the world, like the crown's beautiful container, includes small openings, giving it a quality of wonder integral to being and experience that allows one to sense intuitively what is hidden within the cosmos. The very word for crown— *keter*—is employed in kabbalistic terminology for the highest of the *sefirot,* closest to the boundless infinity of the Divine. In hasidic teaching, it tends to be identified with the *Ein Sof,* the infinite state of the Godhead, unbounded and beyond all definition or conception. The *Ein Sof* is ultimately the sole true reality, which, beyond and within all that exists, gives (relative) being to all else. One must seek to perceive the Divine within and underlying all that is—just as in the parable a wise person must make the effort to perceive the crown within the container.

Hasidic teaching often suggests that the Torah itself, in the concrete written form in which we have it, also bears similarity to a container. The Torah can be understood either on a simple level or on higher levels of interpretation where the same words and letters are understood to carry a much greater depth of meaning and spiritual experience. The Torah is ultimately nothing less than an expression or manifestation of Divinity itself, and therefore it is important to look beneath its surface, which is a kind of container for the deeper meaning concealed within it.

Yitzhak of Radvil points to different expressions of the Divine found in the Torah text. The Jew, reading the Torah, is to proceed beyond the surface conception of God to the depths of the divine reality—the very name of God. Torah and prayer alike are to be understood in terms of the letters that comprise the words but are not bound or limited by the words and their meaning. Those letters represent the divine light and energy that underlie and infuse all of existence. According to Yitzhak of Radvil, a sense of that divine inner dimension of all being—deeper than the more surface-oriented conceptions of the Divine as totally above and apart from humanity—is revealed to those who have been able to rid themselves of all worldly desires.[6]

The container may also suggest Torah study and mitzvot (the commanded deeds of the Torah and its tradition). These comprise the language of the sacred, a language encompassing both texts and deeds. Hasidism affirms that matrix of traditional religious behavior and study. It was never satisfied, however, with the framework alone but rather sought, through mitzvot and Torah study, to focus upon their inner dimension, and to attach oneself to their inner Root, just as the wise person in the parable was not satisfied to see the container but directed his gaze at the crown concealed within it. The early hasidic teachers realized a basic tendency and danger in regarding the holy act as an end in itself and of focusing exclusively upon form. Their criticism represents a countertendency to penetrate beyond the surface aspect of holy acts and of sacred texts in order to connect with their deeper, inner dimension.

Perhaps this parable of Yitzhak of Radvil might serve as the parable par excellence in voicing the core of classical Hasidism. The parable directs the listener to proceed beyond surface perceptions both of the world and of the forms of religious life—the language of the sacred—and to become attuned to a deeper, more inner dimension of both.

1. *Or Yitzhak,* p. 11, Bereshit.
2. Concerning the latter, see Miles Krassen, *Uniter of Heaven and Earth,* pp. 23–31.
3. The region in Poland that, with the divisions of Poland in the late eighteenth century, came to be incorporated into the Austro-Hungarian Empire.
4. M. Avot 4:27.
5. *Likkutim yekarim* (1974), #192.
6. *Or Yitzhak, Derush le-shabbat holo shel mo'ed shel pesah,* pp. 177–181. According to Yitzhak of Radvil, it is that conception and awareness of God with emphasis upon the divine immanence which distinguishes the event of the Revelation at Sinai.

Beyond Request

~

A parable of one who deeply desired to speak with the king, his heart burning with that wish. . . . And it happened that the king decreed that he would fulfill any request made of him. But when this person, who so desired to speak with the king, approached to make his request, he feared lest the king might actually grant him his request. For then he would lack nothing, in which case what reason would he have to speak with the king? And for this reason he actually preferred that the king not grant his request, so that he would have reason to continue to come before the king and speak with him.

And this is the meaning of the verse: "The entire prayer of the afflicted person is that he be able to pour out his heart before the Lord" (the homilist's reading of Ps. 102:1). *(Degel mahane Efrayim)*[1]

The above parable, related by Moshe Hayyim Efrayim of Sedilikov, a grandson of the Baal Shem Tov, raises a question concerning petitionary prayer—prayer in the form of a request. The school of the Maggid of Mezherich[2] taught emphatically that the essence of prayer is not making a request, and if a request is made, it is at most but an occasion for prayer, an excuse to speak with God. The act of making a connection with God far surpasses any request and paradoxically includes all requests. "An unanswered prayer," said Efrayim of Sedilikov, "is a thing of joy." While for Rabbi Nahman of Bratslav, petitioning God for one's needs exemplifies a simplicity and directness in prayer,[3] others, including the Maggid, understood prayer as a liberation from and transcendence of self and its concerns, an emptying of all consciousness of self.

Efrayim's parable is based upon a contradiction between the supplicant's *stated* request and his *real* request. As in relationships between human beings, friends cherish one another not for the tangible benefits they receive from each other but rather because of the ongoing contact and communication built into the friendship. *Personness* takes precedence over *thingness*.

In his homily containing this parable, Efrayim of Sedilikov was seeking to understand a version of the familiar saying of Antigonus of Sokho found in the Mishnah: "Do not be as servants who serve their master in order to receive a reward, but rather be like servants who serve the master not in order to receive a reward."[4] The hasidic homilist cited a different version of that mishnaic saying: "Be like servants who serve their master *on condition that they not receive a reward.*" Efrayim of Sedilikov quoted his grandfather the Baal Shem Tov to explain that both versions are correct but that they represent two different levels, with the latter higher than the former. The parable exemplifies that paradoxical second version in which the servant does his work precisely in order *not* to receive a reward! Reward, it was felt, impugns both one's motivation and one's service.

1. *Degel maḥane Efrayim* (1963), p. 253, *Haftarat tetse.*
2. See Rivka Schatz Uffenheimer, *Hasidism as Mysticism,* chap. 7, "Contemplative Prayer," pp. 168–188.
3. Note *Likkute Moharan,* #14; also *Siḥot Haran,* #233. Also Pinhas of Korets, a member of the circle of the Baal Shem Tov and, hence, a significant figure in the background of early eighteenth-century Hasidism, opposed the Maggid's position concerning contemplative prayer in favor of direct petitionary prayer on the part of the worshiper.
4. M. Avot 1:3.

Sound without Words

~

he following is a wondrous parable that was told before the sounding of the shofar:[1] . . . A king, great and majestic, sends his sons out to hunt. The sons stray from the path and lose their way. They begin shouting, hoping their father might hear, but there is no response. Then they reason: "Perhaps we have forgotten our father's language, and for that reason he does not hear and respond to our shouting. So let us simply shout with sound but without words." And they decide to appoint one of the brothers to engage in shouting, warning him that he must realize that they are all dependent upon him.

The *nimshal* is as follows: The Holy One, blessed be He, sent us to raise up the Holy Sparks, but we strayed from our Father, and later when we shouted to Him, He did not hear us. So now we are unable to pray with language. Instead—[addressing the shofar blower] "we are sending you to awaken compassion for us by sounding the ram's horn, producing sound without any words. And be aware that all of us, men and women alike, are dependent upon you."

"But nonetheless [lest you succumb to pride by reason of the gravity of your responsibility], you must regard yourself as nothing—just like a musical instrument[2] made of skin with holes through which one produces melody. Does the instrument take pride in that sound that proceeds from it? It is similar in the case of a person: one's thought and language and all one's qualities are simply like the holes in such an instrument. Should the one sounding the shofar feel proud? In himself, he [also] is nothing." *(Likkutim yekarim)*[3]

"Our Father's language," by its very nature, goes beyond human language and words, and the recourse to the raw sound of the shofar expresses a realization of the inadequacy of words.

The above parable, which the Maggid of Mezherich himself is said to have related just prior to the sounding of the shofar on Rosh Hashanah, is found also in another text containing his teachings[4] where the context goes on to relate it to the thought that in offering prayer of petition, man is not attuned to God's language. Hence the immediate context of the parable voices the problematic place of petitionary prayer in the spiritual world of much of early Hasidism, especially in the teachings of the Maggid and in his ideational crystallization of Hasidism.

The parable, if read carefully within the context of the Maggid's teachings as a whole, questions not only petitionary prayer but also the assumed role of words in prayer. It cautions the listener against identifying prayer with words. His view of prayer might be understood on its most basic level as an assertion that what God hears is not our words but rather something that happens within the person praying—a deeper dimension of prayer transcending language. Words, the Maggid would claim, while necessary for prayer, are a vehicle to reach beyond the words to activate a deeper aspect of the self. The function of the words of prayer is to allow the person to connect with the innerness of the prayer experience—an experience in which one attains a level that transcends both words and their meaning, as well as awareness of self. To communicate with the Divine, it is necessary—like the sons in the parable story—to transcend language and in that way to reacquire "the language of the Father." While emphasis is placed upon the uttering of the prayer text, the focus in the Maggid's thinking is not upon the words comprising that text but rather upon the very letters that make up the words and upon the spiritual energy identified with the letters. The mental attachment to the letters, in turn, allows the worshiper to attain a level in which the mind is at rest, having attained a higher level of consciousness. The ecstasy of the prayer experience lifts the person beyond the level of language to that of Divine Thought.

The Maggid related his view on language to his reading of the kabbalistic sefirotic world. Speech is associated with *malkhut,* the lowest of the ten *sefirot.* Thought, far transcending speech and language, is associated with *binah,* a higher *sefirah,* which is itself rooted in the still higher *sefirah* of *ḥokhmah,* the level of Divine Thought that transcends human experience. Prayer brings the worshiper to a much deeper point within his own consciousness and to a higher level within the world of the Divine. To the mind of the Maggid, prayer involves essentially a psychological silence, "a silencing of man's speech," a liberation from a person's preoccupation with self and, hence, an act of spiritual transcendence.[5]

When prayer is reduced to uttering words and fails to transcend words, then those same words—even if they are the words of the liturgy—no longer serve as a language of prayer. When prayer does not progress beyond words, the worshiper has forgotten—indeed no longer has access to—the essential language of prayer.

Words assume a place of primacy in prayer. Liturgy is composed of words. In the history of Jewish prayer, silence and spontaneity have often given way to a fixed, spoken liturgy. The recitation of psalms preceding the official morning prayer *(pesuke dezimra),* the penitential prayer *(taḥanun),* and the conclusion of the silent prayer *(Amidah)* each filled what was initially a time for silent and unstructured, contemplative prayer. During the course of time they received a definite linguistic content. The result is both a beautiful liturgy and a crisis of worship as the reciting of words too easily becomes an end in itself without connecting those words with a deeper dimension within the person. And when that happens, we have "forgotten our Father's language."

The recourse to the shofar blasts in the parable—pure sound without words—might suggest to the contemporary reader various other paths aimed at transcending words: the often untapped power of ritual along with melody and chant, both of which can often touch a person on a deeper level than words. Melodies that have a quality of soulness (such as the hasidic *niggun*[6]), or moments of silence or reflection and meditation, are all attempts to liberate prayer from the primacy of uttering words. The equivalent of "sound without words" in the Maggid's parable might be a shout or a whisper; it might be the blast of the shofar or a melody expressing a deep longing that cannot be adequately expressed with words. Perhaps, above all, the contemporary reader might understand in this parable the advantage of a space for silence that surrounds the spoken or chanted word and that restores to the word its allusion to that greater mystery in which we are rooted—the Divine Presence underlying all existence. Then the word might once again become "our Father's language."

The basic motif in the above parable of the Maggid is heard also in the following parable related by one of his students, Rabbi Levi Yitzhak of Berdichev.

A king sent his only son to a distant land for an undisclosed reason. And in the course of time the son became accustomed to living among the villagers there and he lived a wild life as they did. He forgot the ways of the king's court; his mind together with his nature grew coarse and insensitive; and he also forgot the language of his own kingdom. Then one day the son heard that the king was to come to that land where he was living, and when the king came, the son appeared before his father the king and shouted in a loud and strange voice, simply a shout without words, for he had forgotten the king's language. And when the king recognized his son's voice and understood that his son had forgotten his native language, he was overcome with compassion for his son. And this is the reason for the sound of the shofar. (*Kedushat Levi ha-shalem*)[7]

In the Berdichever's parable, the son's having lost his knowledge of the king's language aroused pity in his father. So, it is implied, our inability to communicate with God—our loss of the applicable "language"—and our consequent sounding of the shofar might similarly arouse Divine pity on us.

In the parable told by the Maggid of Mezherich, the warning against pride on the part of the brother sounding the shofar, and by extension on the part of any person engaged in any activity or displaying any talent, recalls an analogy concerning the ram's horn that the Maggid elsewhere related in another context.

> What is heard is [simply] the effect of the person sounding the ram's horn, and were the shofar blower to separate himself from the instrument, no sound whatsoever would be made.
>
> Similarly, apart from God—may He be blessed—a person has no capacity to speak or to think. (*Maggid devarav le-Ya'akov*)[8]

One's words and thought, and even one's prayers, are not really one's own, for a person can no more produce them on his own than an instrument can produce music without the musician. In all that a person does, he or she is like the ram's horn, which in itself is powerless to produce any sound. This realization is essential to true prayer, which, in the teaching of the Maggid, is a total liberation from ego awareness. The one assigned to sound the shofar must understand the meaning of humility from the instrument itself, which experiences no pride in the music it produces since it is incapable of producing any sound on its own. Likewise, we are incapable of doing anything—even thinking, speaking, or praying—without the capacities given to us.

1. The ram's horn sounded on Rosh Hashanah.

2. *Magrefah,* an ancient musical instrument played in the Temple (B. Erakhin 10b), perhaps an early form of the organ.

3. *Likkutim yekarim* (1974), #289.

4. *Or ha-emet* (1899), 7b.

5. See Rivka Schatz Uffenheimer, *Hasidism as Mysticism,* chap. 7, "Contemplative Prayer," pp. 168–188.

6. Essentially, a melody without words. Rabbi Nahman of Bratslav spoke of the *niggun* as a refraction of silence, an allusion to the sublime truth which transcends our words and our thoughts. *Likkute Moharan,* #64.

7. *Kedushat Levi ha-shalem* (1993), p. 490, *Likkutim le-rosh ha-shanah,* with the note that the Berdichever heard this parable, in part, from the holy man Berish. The reader will recognize lines of similarity with the parable told by Rabbi Hayyim of Zanz included in part four of this collection.

8. *Maggid devarav le-Ya'akov* (1976), #106, p. 184. See also *Or ha-emet* (1899), 1b.

On the Language
of Melody

~

A servant who had rebelled against his king and had consequently been banished from the latter's house felt a powerful desire to see his lord and to be reconciled with him and fulfill his will. The guards, however, refused to allow him to enter the king's court. So what does he do? He stands outside and sings songs and praises, and from these songs alone the king will understand the depth of his intent. And hearing the servant's intent as voiced through those songs, the king has mercy upon him and restores him to his court. *(Or Yitzhak)*[1]

Some thoughts and feelings cannot be expressed by everyday language—deep emotions of the kind that require that one go beyond the realm of direct, conventional discourse. In the homily that includes the above parable, Yitzhak of Radvil discusses the songs and praises recited on the festival of Pesaḥ (Passover) that refer to the mutual love between God and the people of Israel. The homilist recalls the idea, found in classical rabbinic lore,[2] that the people of Israel arose in God's thought even prior to the creation of the world, an idea that implies—to the mind of Yitzhak of Radvil—a relationship that cannot be expressed in any language—including Hebrew. Such love transcends all direct formulation in words and is indeed beyond the reach of words and language. Yitzhak of Radvil ascribes to the Men of the Great Assembly[3] not only the foundations of historical Jewish worship but also the more subtle mode of worship through song and poetry based largely on allusion.[4] The phenomenon of such poetic expression—more akin to the language of the soul—is explained in the premise that "God wants the heart."[5]

The extended explication of the parable by Yitzhak of Radvil, as found in the text, suggests that the parable may not have had its origins in this homily. Rather, the master may have been drawing from another source or from a known parable, perhaps from a parable that he himself had created for another context and then transferred to the homily in which the parable is now situated. The reader will note a basic discrepancy between the *mashal* and the *nimshal*. The parable story speaks of a servant and his master, while the extended explication comprises a love narrative concerning a man and a woman. The liturgical poems recited during the prayers of Pesaḥ as well as the passages referring to sacrificial offerings are interpreted in the context of their love narrative.

In his *nimshal* of the parable, Yitzhak of Radvil explains that God took Israel as a wife after she alone was willing to draw near to the *avodah* (worship in an all-inclusive sense) of God who sought, from among all the nations, one people who would accept the Torah and thus be, as it were, God's spouse. The homilist recognizes two sides of the process of choosing as he asks, "Who is seeking whom" in this love relationship? The festival of Pesaḥ served as the bridegroom's gift to his bride (according to legal custom). As a gift given in love, the inner joy of the festival is inexpressible in everyday, prosaic language.

The *nimshal* becomes, in effect, another *mashal* in which Israel remains loyal to their mutual love even during the experience of exile. To console her, God then gives to Israel His recollections of the period of Israel's afflictions. As an allegory of history, the new parable now speaks of a king who, under pressure from members of his wife's court who are envious of her, sends his queen away to a foreign land after she commits some misdeed and repents. The king remembers her lovingkindness to him, in that she alone was willing to accept and marry him; but he cannot annul the royal decree, already issued, sending her into exile. So the king goes into exile with her in order to protect her, and afterwards he joyfully restores her to their home. Continuing his parable, the reader learns that due to the intensity of her love, the years of affliction have vanished from her mind, and for this reason the king writes down his memories of that period, giving them to her to comfort her.

It would follow that not only the *piyyutim* (the liturgical poems) of the Pesaḥ festival speak the language of love and can be understood only in the context of that love relationship, but the very festival itself and the biblical account of oppression in bondage and deliverance from Egypt can be read only through the lens of that love narrative.

The statement of the inner meaning of history that Yitzhak of Radvil presents here would be incompatible with the tenor of Maimonides, who employed the criterion of a universally understandable logic. Yitzhak's views are more akin to the existential position of Yehudah ha-Levi, for whom love and relationship are not limited by universal modes of reason, but can be understood and voiced only through the subjectivity of song and poetry.

---

1. *Or Yitzhak, Derush le-ḥolo shel mo'ed pesaḥ,* p. 180.
2. *Midrash bereshit rabbah* 1:4.
3. A body of sages said to function at some point during the Second Commonwealth.
4. *Or Yitzhak,* pp. 179–180.
5. B. Sanhedrin 106b.

When Truth Confronts Limited Understanding

∽

A father sees his son playing with walnuts, and out of his love for him, the father himself joins in the child's game, even though to the father this seems like a very childish thing. Nevertheless due to his love for his son and his wish to experience delight in him, the father contracts his profound intelligence and he behaves in a seemingly juvenile way, which the young child is capable of understanding and to which he can relate. If, however, the father were to relate to the child according to the father's own level of intelligence, the son would be totally incapable of understanding. *(Maggid devarav le-Ya'akov)*[1]

The above parable as told by the Maggid, Dov Baer of Mezherich, and repeated in numerous variations in the Maggid's homilies and comments, is present also in a parable related by one of his students, Levi Yitzhak of Berdichev:

> If a very young child speaks any word of wisdom at all, the father is delighted in the child's words, even though the intelligence of the father is far greater—much beyond the grasp of the child. Nevertheless, because of the father's love for his young child, he retreats from his

own level of mind and seemingly contracts his intelligence to the level of the child in order to experience
pleasure with him, and he ignores his own infinitely
higher level of intelligence. *(Kedushat Levi ha-shalem)*[2]

The above parables allude to two seemingly contradictory images of
the Divine: both a highly abstract sense of the Infinite Godhead, beyond
the grasp of the human mind, and the image of a tender child's loving
father. The combination of these two direct the listener to the idea that
each level of being is, in itself, incomprehensible to the level beneath it.
Consequently the truth of the higher worlds—and in particular the highest of the four kabbalistic levels of being *(atzilut)*—so transcends the
reaches of the human mind that its truth must be radically contracted to
enable a human being to grasp it to any extent at all. It must be radically
altered to allow for human comprehension, which is limited by its very
nature. One might extend the analogy and consider the gulf between
human mentality and that of the animal world: what can an animal, even
a household pet, comprehend concerning human intellectual activity?

The Maggid explains that the level of Moses was higher than that of the
other Prophets, and he suggests further that every person attains a different level of understanding. "As a person appears when standing before a
mirror, so the image in the mirror will appear to him; it is similar, if one
can so speak, in regard to the Holy One, blessed be He: as a person shows
himself before Him, may He be blessed, so does He appear to him."[3] In
one passage from his teachings, the Maggid explains a statement from
rabbinic aggadah maintaining that at the Reed Sea the Israelites imagined
God to be a youth, while at Sinai they imagined him as an elderly wise
man.[4] He then supplies the *nimshal* to this aggadic comment. The
Israelites, in fact, perceived God as a reflection or image of themselves at
that particular stage of their development. Leaving Egypt, they were on a
mental level comparable to a youth. Progressing through their experiences in the desert while proceeding toward Mount Sinai, they became
much more fully developed. God did not change, but the mindset of the
Israelites changed from one stage to the next, and so they depicted God

in their minds differently as they themselves ascended from one level to a higher level. Their perceptions of the Divine were, in reality, a kind of mirror image of themselves, and those perceptions conveyed nothing concerning the Divine but everything about themselves.[5]

In any such situation, God contracts Himself to accommodate the particular level of the person, according to each person's mental and spiritual ability to grasp His being. By nature we are all as young children, playing with walnuts, in our necessarily limited grasp of the reality of God.

Rabbi Levi Yitzhak of Berdichev connected his parable with the opening words of the *Zikhronot* ("Remembrances"), the second of the three sections of the *Musaf* (the "Additional Prayer Service"), which are unique to Rosh Hashanah. The beginning of the introduction to *Zikhronot* might be translated: "You remember happenings from the beginning of time and You bring to Your mind all that was created in the earliest times." The Berdichever explains the last phrase as a reference to *atzilut* (the highest of the four realms in the kabbalistic view of the cosmos), and—on the basis of I Samuel 20:25—he understood the verb *poked* (usually understood as "remember") to mean "decrease." Hence, "You decrease the higher truth of Your Divine Reality and make room within the utter infinity of Your thought for what transpires at our level of existence." The theme emerging from the Berdichever's rather complicated exegesis of that verse from the *Zikhronot* is voiced more simply and clearly in his parable.

Both of the above parables imply that all our conceptions of the Divine are on the level of the child's very limited way of thinking. Given the inherent limitations of the human mind, the human being is always a child vis-à-vis the Divine Truth, and a person necessarily grasps that truth in a way that mirrors the limitations of his or her own mental and spiritual state. And yet the greater divine reality accommodates itself to the limitations of our comprehension, and God enters, so to speak, into the images fostered by our own imagination.

The masters of the hasidic parable saw in the young child an appropriate example of the limitations of human understanding. Recognizing that parallel, it is necessary to understand one's own mental images of God as being limited, just as a young child cannot grasp what transcends his capacity to understand.

1. *Maggid devarav le-Ya'akov* (1976), #132, p. 229.
2. *Kedushat Levi ha-shalem* (1993), *le-rosh ha-shanah,* p. 278.
3. *Maggid devarav le-Ya'akov* (1976), #132, p. 228. The mirror image in the Maggid's parable echoes much earlier utilization of the mirror image found in the writings of Rabbi Moshe Cordovero (see Berakha Zack, *Besha'are ha-kabbalah shel rabbi Moshe Cordovero,* pp. 205–213; also "Rabbi Moshe Cordovero's Influence upon Hasidism," pp. 233–234). It is also popular in medieval literature, especially in Sufi philosophical writings (Hava Lazarus-Yafeh, *Studies in* Al-Ghazzali, pp. 312–315, "The Parable of the Mirror").
4. *Mekhilta derabbi Yishma'el,* Yitro, #5.
5. *Maggid devarav le-Ya'akov* (1976), #164, pp. 264–265.

When a House of Sticks
Is Shattered

⟜

A parable of the king's young child who constructed for himself a small house of little twigs, as young children are accustomed to do. . . . A man comes along and shatters that house that the king's child has made. The young child comes to his father complaining and crying before him concerning his great distress brought about by that man. But hearing this, the father laughs, even though he loves his child very much. For in the father's eyes that little house of twigs is worthless compared with the good things his father intends to prepare for him, for he has it in mind to build for his son large and beautiful palaces. And this poor, lowly structure means nothing at all in his eyes that he should take vengeance against the man who knocked it down, and even though it brought great distress to the child, the father gives no attention to it. To the mind of the child it is a distressful thing, but his father knows that much greater goods are destined for him. (*Likkutim yekarim*)[1]

The Maggid of Mezherich brings two very different perspectives into comparison in this parable. The human and divine perspectives are represented respectively by that of a young child and of a mature parent. The child is unable to understand his father's indifference, even to the point of mocking the son's plight. The two vantage points are never bridged within the parable story. The child will of course never understand, but the reader, having access to a larger perspective, is able to comprehend the mind of the parent.

The parable relates to all the normal concerns in life that seem so crucial to individuals. When viewed from a higher perspective, however, these problems are reduced to the level of a child's game. Human distress is likened to the suffering of a child when his house of twigs is overturned.

The *nimshal* explains that the child represents the *tzaddik* (holy man) whose prayers regarding the things of this world go unanswered and appear to be ignored. The Maggid makes the paradoxical assertion that such prayers are unanswered precisely as a mark of God's affection for the *tzaddik*. The key to the paradox is that all worldly concerns and even one's distress in this world cannot compare with the good awaiting the holy ones in the world to come, "for all the good of this world is as nothing when compared to the powerful love in the wake of which he will receive the concealed goodness of the world to come."

The Maggid consistently disparages concern with worldly matters and with one's situation in life. And while the *nimshal* mentions the blessings stored up for a person in the world to come—a conventional explanation in Jewish tradition—in the broader context of the Maggid's thinking there is no real importance attached to reward or expectation of reward in the world to come.[2] One's motivation in life and in serving God must be free from any expression of self-concern or an expectation of personal gain. The father responds with indifference to the child's distress for he knows that in an ultimate sense it lacks significance.

---

1. *Likkutim yekarim* (1974), #164.
2. See Rivka Schatz Uffenheimer, *Hasidism as Mysticism*, p. 81.

The Suffering of the Shekhinah

⤳

A woman had an only child very beloved to her, and once when that son committed a serious sin against the king, the king ordered that he be chastised with sufferings inflicted upon him. His mother, in utter disillusion, would painfully see her son's afflictions, and the son told her, "Mother, know that I do not feel at all the pains caused by the whippings because I have sufferings much greater than those lashes—namely, knowing that you witness my sufferings. Your own distress from my lashes is much graver to me than the pain caused by the lashes themselves."

During that time, he began to cry out to the king, "Spare me, my lord; let go of me and allow me to speak with you." He then said to the king, "I do not ask that you forgive me for my iniquity or that you cease inflicting sufferings upon me, for truthfully I deserve them. Only this I request of you. You are certainly a truthful judge who acts out of unblemished integrity. Therefore wouldn't it be possible for you to inflict me with sufferings without making my mother suffer through my distress? Were it not for the sorrow my mother experiences, I would gladly and lovingly accept my own sufferings. Her distress, however, gives me pain much more than does my own distress. Do this for the sake of my mother, for she has not sinned." And the king answered, "I will do so for her sake." *(Turei zahav)* [1]

The above parable, related by Binyamin ben Aharon of Zalozetz, though stylistically different from the more specifically hasidic type of parable we have been reading, voices a significant theme in early hasidic thought: in prayer a person must be concerned neither with his own needs nor his own distress, but rather with the distress experienced by the Shekhinah, resulting from one's misdeeds. To the Maggid and his followers, including Binyamin of Zalozetz, giving thought to one's own problems or needs is incompatible with the contemplative nature of prayer. It follows, then, that if traditional prayer contains an element of petition, it should concern not one's own needs but rather the Divine suffering—the exile of the Shekhinah.

This parable exemplifies both a distancing from one's personal distress in life and a depth of empathy with the Divine who is not above suffering. As the Maggid himself made very clear, "One should not pray concerning his own personal needs but rather only for the plight of the Shekhinah that it find redemption from exile." [2]

The parable itself is quite transparent. The mother represents the Shekhinah, both in the more general sense of the Divine Presence—the Divine in its more immanent state most closely bound up with the world and its experience—and the specific kabbalistic meaning of the tenth and lowest of the *sefirot*, (aspects of the Godhead). Kabbalistic teaching speaks of the captivity of the Shekhinah at the hands of the evil and impure forces countering the divine reality and its suffering in being severed from the higher *sefirot*, including *tiferet* (a distinctly masculine *sefirah*). The latter conception is a kabbalistic interpretation of an earlier rabbinic conception of the Shekhinah's departure from the Temple and from the Land of Israel in order to accompany Her children in their exile. Not only Israel, but also God experiences exile, though in the earlier rabbinic conception, the Shekhinah goes into exile as an act of choice.

It should be evident to the reader that the Divine, in this parable, is characterized not by power but rather by the suffering it bears largely as a consequence of human action and events. A distinctly feminine *sefirah,* the Shekhinah is regarded as a maternal figure to the people Israel—a mother who shares in the distress of Israel most poignantly.[3]

This parable can be understood as part of a parable tradition found in the Zohar that contrasts the masculine aspect of Divinity—seemingly distant and lacking in compassion—with the empathetic feminine dimension of Divinity represented by the Shekhinah. In such parables, the father punishes his own son following the latter's transgressions, which exceed his father's tolerance, while the mother, married (or once married) to the king, bears the burden of excessive suffering while feeling nothing but compassion for her son.[4] Perhaps only with an eye for that broader background of the parable can one understand the conclusion: the father, though not perceived initially as having compassion, agrees not to cause distress to the son's mother, for she is also his wife.

This parable voices the need to transcend one's own personal needs and distress and to cultivate instead an empathy with the pain of the One who transcends us and our experience. It reflects, in addition, a sense of oneself as a limb of the Divine Presence. By implication, as though allowing a way for self-concern to reenter through the back door, if the Shekhinah is able to experience joy and wholeness, those qualities will extend also to all of its limbs.[5]

---

1. *Turei zahav* (1989), *Derush le-yom ha-kippurim,* p. 253.
2. *Maggid devarav le-Ya'akov* (1976), #12, p. 25.
3. See Aryeh Wineman, *Mystic Tales from the Zohar,* pp. 10–12; Aryeh Wineman, *Beyond Appearances,* pp. 140–145. On the suffering of the Shekhinah, see also Nehemiah Polen, *The Holy Fire,* chap. 6, "The Mystical Vision of Divine Weeping," pp.106–121, which examines Rabbi Kalonymus Kalman Shapira's relationship to this theme of divine suffering as a response to the tragic experience of Jews in the Warsaw Ghetto during World World II.
4. See Zohar 2:189a.
5. *Maggid devarav le-Ya'akov* (1976), #32, pp. 51–52.

Unconventional Ways
to Serve

⌒

When people wish to give a present to a king of flesh and blood, even if they bring him all the gifts in the world—beautiful objects made of gold and silver and pearls—all these would be of no significance in the eyes of the king. Would they add anything new to what the king already possesses? Has the king no gold or silver or pearls or precious stones in his personal treasury? Even an infant understands that though these gifts are of great worth and beauty, there is no value in bringing to the king what he already possesses.

This is not the case, however, when people draw upon their wisdom and prepare attractive and decorative objects from a clod of earth, fashioning from it exceedingly lovely paintings so that all who see them would experience joy in their inner being and would exclaim, "This is a new creation, an innovation accomplished by persons of skill who have the ability to fashion such lovely objects and instruments from a clod of earth. Such objects are not even found within the royal treasury." *(Or ha-me'ir)*[1]

Quoting his teacher, the Maggid of Mezherich, Ze'ev Wolff of Zhitomir explains in the above parable that when one wishes to offer a

gift to God, "to adorn the Shekhinah with decorations," gifts in the form
of Torah study and prayer are not highly treasured in God's eyes insofar
as they are already found in the king's storehouse "in works of inestimable value." Much more preferable are those gifts of true brightness
clad in the lower levels of being. And when one draws up a Holy Spark
from the substance and fabric of everyday life and makes of it a decora-
tion to embellish the Shekhinah, the Holy One, blessed be He, has infinitely greater joy and delight.[2]

If Holy Sparks are found in all of life and all of being—the subject of
the particular homily that includes this parable—then it follows that all
of life's normal pursuits and activities are potentially holy. God delights
in man serving Him in all potential ways, in every aspect of life including
those "secular" aspects that are not typically considered sacred. Eliciting
holiness through secular life is on a level equal to, or, according to the
above parable, higher than, the gifts formed from that sphere of life set off
and designated in people's minds as sacred.

The parable, with its explication, neither negates nor denigrates the
hallowed paths of prayer and Torah study and their place in the comprehensive worship of God. The reader recognizes the preciousness of these
paths as being "of inestimable value" and having their accorded place in
the royal treasury. In themselves, however, prayer and Torah study do
not comprise the totality of the worship of God. Without negating the
accepted hallowed ways,[3] holiness assumes many forms, and all of life
consists of potential ways of serving and worshiping God; in every aspect
of life, it is possible for man to serve God, to respond to and come near
to the Divine. For this reason the gifts to be directed to God—the ways
by which we can draw near to God—can never be fully defined or delineated.

Drawing upon the earlier kabbalistic concept, Ze'ev Wolff of Zhitomir
interprets the Exodus from Egypt in terms of the redemption of fallen
Holy Sparks that, if not elevated and redeemed, continue to suffer exile.
Such sparks—holy in nature insofar as they are manifestations of the
Light of the Infinite Godhead—descended into the abyss with the
Shattering of the Vessels that were unable to contain the Divine Light.
The sparks, calling out to man to redeem them, occupy various levels of
the abyss of being into which they fell with that primordial catastrophe.

The homilist explains that those sparks that are on relatively higher levels can be elevated and redeemed through acts specifically defined as mitzvot (commanded deeds), including prayer and Torah study. Sparks occupying lower levels, however, and hence those in most dire need of redemption, are not elevated in acts conventionally delineated as elements in the path of holiness. These sparks parallel aspects of life that are not normally considered to be within the perimeter of holy living, and these can be redeemed only through acts beyond those spelled out and accepted as hallowed ways. Ze'ev Wolff of Zhitomir emphatically viewed such deeds as bringing greater delight to God.[4]

The verse from Proverbs so often reiterated in early hasidic texts, "Know Him in all your ways" (Prov. 3:6), was understood as an expansion of the concept of service or worship of God to include all that a person does in life. In this vein, it is taught that "God desires that we serve Him *in all ways*." Furthermore, it is for this reason, we read, that there are times when a person finds himself unable to study or to pray, when a person must of necessity be engaged in distracting pursuits such as going on a journey or simply conversing with people, for God takes delight in a person's serving Him *in all ways*, including the less conventionally holy ways.[5]

Viewing all of life as the potential field of holy acts, the conception voiced in this parable represents an aspect of hasidic teaching and spiritual insight that fell victim to the success of Hasidism and was generally abandoned with the flourishing of that movement. With the formation of relatively large communities around a *tzaddik* (the holy man and center of a hasidic community), such revolutionary paths were held to be of relevance only for the *tzaddik*, while his followers were expected instead merely to observe the established, well-trodden ways. For them, the quest for more unconventional and undelineated paths of divine service was, in fact, to be avoided.[6]

---

1. *Or ha-me'ir*, (1995), I, *Derush le-pesaḥ*, pp. 254–255.
2. Ibid., p. 255.
3. Implicitly, however, the conception of unlimited and undefined mitzvot might create a tension with normative tradition by planting doubt concerning the status of those acts

specifically defined by tradition as mitzvot. Both critics of Hasidism and its followers may have sensed in the broadening of the concept of mitzvot a threat to tradition, and perhaps for the same reason even the adherents of Hasidism distanced themselves from and abandoned the openness voiced in the parable of Ze'ev Wolff of Zhitomir. See Arthur Green, "Hasidism," pp. 125–126.

4. Op. cit., *Or ha-me'ir.*
5. *Likkutim yekarim* (1974), #180.
6. See Miles Krassen, *Uniter of Heaven and Earth*, pp. 212, 214.

On the Need for the
Spontaneous

◡

On a well-traveled road, known to all, murderers and highwaymen act at will because they know in advance the route on which people will travel. But when people journey instead along a new path that is not commonly known, the thieves are unable to lie in wait to ambush them. *(Likkute Moharan tinyana)*[1]

Rabbi Nahman of Bratslav was keenly cognizant of the danger of routine and repetition in the life of prayer—the danger of prayer becoming perfunctory and mindless. He spoke of such prayer as being captive to a demonic force that situates itself along a well-traveled route, ready to capture the words of prayer. It was obvious to him that holy acts such as prayer are not immune from being captured by the demonic. Once something is established and made into a repetitive practice, there is a real danger of that element taking over and robbing the act—in this case, prayer—of its very integrity and soul. The spiritual route that is known and marked out in advance, like the main highway, is prey to that danger, with the result that it can lack the quality of a fresh inner experience on the part of the devotee.

Rabbi Nahman was especially concerned with the difficulty of maintaining the desired mindfulness and inner intent in prayer, and he understood the obstacles that stood in the path of such inner devotion (*kavvanah*) in prayer. At the same time, he also exhibited a strong measure of patience, realizing that the human makeup is highly complex, and that despite all the distractions from true prayer and the factor of questionable motivation, there is nonetheless an often-concealed core of pure intent in a person's praying.[2] Along with this, he nevertheless lamented the possibility that prayer itself can be in a state of exile.[3]

In contrast to the previous parable by Ze'ev Wolff of Zhitomir, Nahman provided a specific prescription for resolving that dilemma: spontaneous, individual prayer (siḥah)—personal, intimate, and direct conversation with God. This was Rabbi Nahman's own personal practice from his early years and one that he mandated for his followers. The siḥah corresponds to the new path "not commonly known" to highwaymen who otherwise would seize man's prayer and hold it captive; for, being spontaneous, the siḥah is necessarily a new prayer.

Rabbi Nahman required that each of his followers spend at least an hour each day in solitude (hitbodedut), pouring out one's soul before God, preferably at night, in a location where the sounds of human activity cannot be heard even during the day, and whenever possible outdoors, in a field or in the woods.[4] Interestingly, he related the word siḥah to the word si'aḥ (shrub) to suggest that the ideal setting for such personal, spontaneous prayer is in a natural setting where the grass and shrubs enter into one's prayer.[5] He also suggested a special room for hitbodedut, but lacking such opportunity, one might also simply place his tallit (prayer shawl) over his eyes in order to close out the world and be alone with God.[6]

During that hour of spontaneous prayer in solitude, an hour devoted to contemplative soul searching and to regret, a person can honestly reflect upon his life, enabling him to protect and preserve his own integrity from the threatening influences surrounding him. Hitbodedut can allow for that shattering of one's ego, which is a prerequisite of true prayer. And it can allow a person to judge himself and his activities in life, "to consider whether they are worthy of devoting one's life to them . . . because if a person does not devote time to contemplate, he lacks understanding and will not grasp the foolishness of the world."[7]

This practice of hitbodedut (spontaneous prayer in solitude) in one's mother tongue was not intended as a substitute for the established, traditional liturgical prayer, although Rabbi Nahman spoke of solitary, unstructured prayer with decidedly more emphasis. He regarded it both as preceding formal prayer historically and as retaining a higher value even after the development of the accepted liturgy was already a fact. In his analysis, based partly upon Maimonides, he attempted to place Jewish liturgy in historical perspective locating its source in spontaneous individual prayer.[8] Without annulling anything of the traditional form and practice of prayer, Rabbi Nahman added a new focal point for his own prayer life and for that of his followers.

Rabbi Nahman's demand that his followers engage daily and intensively in such prayer and contemplation in solitude exemplified his tendency to set high spiritual expectations for his followers. Conversely, he was impatient with the intensifying institutionalization of Hasidism during his lifetime and the failure of the emerging hasidic courts to make serious spiritual demands of their followers.[9] With the rapid flourishing of Hasidism among Eastern European Jewry, the masses of followers tended to rely spiritually upon their bond with the holy man (tzaddik). However, Rabbi Nahman insisted upon the spiritual responsibility and the spiritual experience of each person, and he would emphasize that every person, irrespective of status, is capable of serious personal, spontaneous prayer. In more contemporary parlance, Rabbi Nahman was suggesting the dire need for a place for personal voice in the total prayer life of the Jew.[10]

1. *Likkute Moharan tinyana,* #97.
2. *Sihot Haran,* #72.
3. *Likkute Moharan tinyana,* #1.
4. *Likkute Moharan tinyana,* #24, 25, and 96; *Shivhe Moharan,* "Ma'alat ha-hitbodedut," #2.
5. *Likkute Moharan tinyana,* #1; also #11.
6. Quoted in *Hishtaphut ha-nefesh* (1978), #39, p. 43.
7. *Sihot Haran,* #47.
8. *Sihot Haran* #229. Also *Likkute Moharan tinyana,* #120. Rabbi Nahman's reference to Maimonides is to the latter's *Mishneh Torah, Hilkhot tefillah,* 1:1–4.
9. Arthur Green, *Tormented Master,* p. 94ff.
10. The roots of Rabbi Nahman's conception of *hitbodedut* (devotion in solitude) can be traced to both *Me'irat einayim* and *Otzar ha-hayyim* by the late thirteenth- and early fourteenth-century thinker Yitzhak ben Shmuel of Acre (Fenton, 1981, p. 63), an important influence on the thought of Rabbi Moshe Cordovero who, in turn, had a decisive impact on hasidic thought. The vocabulary of Yitzhak ben Shmuel of Acre, in connection with *hitbodedut,* reveals the influence of Sufism and the Sufi practice of *halwa* (ibid.; also note Efrayim Gottlieb, 1969).

The Miraculous within the Everyday

~

I t is not nearly so remarkable that a king triumphs in war when he comes with a multitude of soldiers as when the king is seen in the forest all alone, with no weapons and no soldiers with him, and he is victorious solely by virtue of his own personal heroism.

Similarly, when the king comes to the royal palace, and people witness his glory and see his servants carrying out his will, fearful and embarrassed to disobey him—that is not as remarkable as when the king is alone in the woods, not clad in his royal apparel and having no soldiers present who fear him and are embarrassed not to follow his orders. *(Kedushat Levi ha-shalem)* [1]

The subject of miracles is a frequent topic of discussion in the homilies of Rabbi Levi Yitzhak of Berdichev, and a glance at his treatment of the subject is helpful in understanding the larger context of the above parable.

In those discussions, the Berdichever built upon a basic distinction between overt miracles that are manifest and obvious to all, for example, the Splitting of the Reed Sea and the giving of the manna—actions that alter the natural course of things—and concealed miracles appearing as natural and normal happenings rather than as supernatural acts. That basic distinction—already alluded to in rabbinic sources [2] and spelled out much more systematically in the writings of Nahmanides [3]—received special emphasis in the homilies of Rabbi Levi Yitzhak.

Some of his statements scattered throughout the volume *Kedushat Levi ha-shalem* voice a rather conventional attitude, placing emphasis upon the striking, overt miracles recounted in the Bible, miracles traditionally thought to possess a higher degree of holiness. Other passages, however, suggest a contrasting hierarchy with a distinct preference for concealed miracles over those that alter the natural pattern of things. In fact many of the Berdichever's statements even suggest a disdain for overt miracles. In reading a hasidic homily, statements of a more conventional nature might be seen to reflect the general climate of belief and are in the nature of the expected, while less conventional nuances in the teachings of a master presumably point to his own more personal attitudes and reveal his own convictions.

The Berdichever's preference for "concealed miracles" is voiced in a number of his parables, which place overt miraculous action on a lower plane than the Divine's functioning through the "natural." Overt miracles are said to represent a Divine Retreat from a truer and more exalted state of Divine Wisdom for the purpose, as it were, of communicating with a young child of limited comprehension. Miracles that alter the pattern of nature, he claimed, are equivalent to a contraction (*tzimtzum*) of God's higher intelligence—a descent from His true level.[4] His view of miracles differs from statements of his teacher, the Maggid of Mezherich,[5] and others such as Rabbi Ya'akov Yosef of Polonnoye,[6] which extol obvious miraculous acts as exemplifying a higher level, whereas unnoticed miracles are said to reflect either the unworthiness of the generation or Israel's condition in exile. Overt miracles, the Berdichever suggests, speak to people of a lower mental spiritual grasp or to those who are temporarily in such a lower condition,[7] whereas a person attaining to an expansion of mind[8] arrives at faith through intuition without basing his faith on such overt supernatural miracles. For him, overt miracles have importance only in the event that he might later descend to a lower level of spiritual awareness.[9]

The Berdichever's preference is expressed most emphatically in his discussion of the reading of the Scroll of Esther on Purim. That biblical text contrasts with the Torah account of the Exodus and the wilderness period in that it depicts salvation as coming through a pattern of natural events—a note voiced already by the Maharal of Prague[10]—events in which human beings are the direct actors. In light of that fact, Rabbi Levi Yitzhak placed the miracle of Purim (which occurred seemingly without

any explicit action on God's part) on a higher level than the overt type of
miracle celebrated in the Pesaḥ festival. Building upon a talmudic statement that in the days of Esther and Mordecai, Israel accepted the Torah
a second time,[11] he explains that in the wake of the events described in
the Scroll of Esther, Israel at that time chose to accept the Torah out of
love with a purity of motivation, which is not really compatible with the
manifestation of Divine Power in overt, supernatural acts. Utilizing a
number of rabbinic citations,[12] the Berdichever maintained that the reading of the Scroll of Esther is the subject of greater stringency than is the
reading of the Torah Scroll, and that it takes precedence over the study of
Torah. The Berdichever connected that higher status assigned to the
Scroll of Esther with the importance of the kind of miracle that occurs
within the natural pattern of events.[13] Because the miracle of Purim was
concealed within the natural, Levi Yitzhak maintained that it was even
greater than the miracles in the days of Moses,[14] and that the world of
nature, which through the reading of the Scroll of Esther is elevated to a
more exalted state, glistens in that person who reads it.[15]

In another comparison of Jewish festivals, Pesaḥ (which is based on
overt miraculous deeds) is associated with a limited spiritual grasp and
with serving God in order to receive a reward, whereas the festival of
Shavuot (the Feast of Weeks, commemorating the Giving of the Torah),
representing a higher level of intelligence and awareness, exemplifies service to God for God's sake, with no consideration of reward. The
Berdichever relates this comparison to the tradition found in a midrashic
source that, whereas at the Exodus, God appeared to the Israelites as a
very young man, at Sinai the Israelites perceived God instead as a mature,
compassionate sage.[16] At Sinai both the spiritual state of the people and
the nature of the event were of a higher character, distanced from overt
miracle.[17]

In the *nimshal* of the above parable, Levi Yitzhak goes on to compare
the situation of the king unaccompanied by evidence of power and
authority to Israel's acceptance of the Torah out of a purity of motivation
in the days of Esther and Mordecai. In the latter instance, God's actions
were not overt but rather hidden from view. In contrast, he claims
that the acceptance of the Torah in a context of overt divine deeds that
alter nature—the context of miracles described in the biblical account

of the Exodus and the wilderness period—occupies a lower level.

The Berdichever maintained that all natural events are really miracles, negating a conception of the world functioning according to a fixed pattern of regularity.[18] While never denying the actual occurrence of overt miracles—stating, in fact, that believing in both types of miracles brings one to a conception of the Oneness of God encompassing both kinds[19]— his rather constant deflation of the importance of overt supernatural miracles might be seen to reflect two basic beliefs. One is the hasidic emphasis upon the immanence of the Divine concealed within the seemingly natural and ordinary. "There is no place devoid of the Divine; even within the natural, [God] accomplishes for us miracles and wonders, clad within what is natural."[20] Rabbi Levi Yitzhak even suggests that the word *megillah* (scroll), in reference to the Scroll of Esther, connects with the concealed state of God's kingship within natural things, the scroll disclosing *(megallah)* the hidden miracle.[21] Perhaps more than any of the other early hasidic thinkers and in contradiction to some, the Berdichever refracts the subject of miracles through the lens of that hasidic emphasis on divine immanence and its implications. With his insistence upon the sense of the miracle in seemingly natural events, overt miracle becomes superfluous.

A second factor, perhaps even more important, is Levi Yitzhak's distinct sense that the overtly miraculous blemishes and even contradicts human freedom of choice and response. In this vein, he suggests that God did not give the Torah to the Israelites immediately upon their leaving Egypt for the reason that their memory of overt miracles such as the Splitting of the Sea was still very much alive in their consciousness. Their acceptance of the Torah under such conditions would have appeared to be in return for having received overt divine favors. Instead, God waited until the memory of the events of the Exodus had dimmed in their consciousness and their thought focused instead on their needs and hardships and they began to complain. Only then was their acceptance of the Torah unblemished, rooted solely in their love.[22] True service, worship, and obedience to God, the Berdichever insisted, must flow from a true freedom of response, not from coercion; and an overt, supernatural miracle can easily have the effect of coercion. The capacity for human choice is possible only when God's power is not evident.[23]

The following brief parable of Rabbi Levi Yitzhak of Berdichev exemplifies the crucial significance of freedom of response in the Berdichever's teachings.

> When a servant serves his master, there is nothing remarkable in his service, for he lacks the choice and prerogative not to serve him, and for this reason the master does not receive any unusual delight from his service. This is not the case, however, with his beloved son who has the choice whether or not to serve his father. *(Kedushat Levi ha-shalem)*[24]

In the textual context of this parable, the Berdichever points out that because angels—like the royal servants in the *mashal*—lack freedom of choice, God takes infinitely greater delight when worshiped by those who also have the very real possibility of not serving Him. In this vein, Levi Yitzhak comments that it is the very presence of the Evil Inclination (the *yetzer ha-ra*) in man that allows for a condition of choice and that is therefore a necessary factor in determining whether service to God is true or automatic and meaningless. One cannot really grasp the Berdichever's views on miracles without noting his concern for a condition of freedom of choice and response.

While hasidic tales abound in supernatural miracles and wonders, one notes within the homilies of Rabbi Levi Yitzhak of Berdichev, and occasionally also in the words of other hasidic masters, nuances of an emphatic devaluation of overt miracles. The coexistence of these contradictory temperaments is a mark of the complexity of Hasidism as a religious and cultural phenomenon.

---

1. *Kedushat Levi ha-shalem* (1993), *Kedushah rishonah*, pp. 337–338.
2. See Ephraim A. Urbach, *Ḥazal: emunot ve-de'ot*, pp. 92–95. Note also the *modim* in the *Amidah*, "Your miracles and wonders which we experience daily, each evening, morning and noon. . . ."
3. Moses ben Nahman [1194–1270]. See *Ramban: Writings and Discourses*, vol. 1, pp. 69–71.

4. *Kedushat Levi ha-shalem* (1993), *Derush le-pesaḥ,* p. 181. The more general concept of the contraction of Divine Wisdom to accommodate the limitations of human understanding is a recurrent theme in the teachings of Levi Yitzhak's teacher, the Maggid, Dov Baer of Mezherich.

5. *Maggid devarav le-Ya'akov* (1976), #14, 35; *Likkutim yekarim* (1974), #29.

6. *Toledot Ya'akov Yosef* (1973), p. 177, Be-shallaḥ.

7. "*Moḥin de-katnut.*" *Kedushat Levi ha-shalem, Kelalot ha-nissim,* p. 401.

8. *Moḥin de-gadlut.*

9. *Kedushat Levi ha-shalem, Derush le-pesaḥ,* p. 181.

10. *Or ḥadash,* Introduction.

11. B. Shabbat 88a.

12. From B. Megillah 3b.

13. *Kedushat Levi ha-shalem, Kedushah rishonah,* p. 339.

14. Ibid., p. 337.

15. Ibid., p. 339.

16. Ibid., p. 136, Yitro. The aggadic statement is found in *Mekhilta derabbi Yishma'el,* Yitro, #5, and also in *Pesikta rabbati, piska* 21, trans. William G. Braude, vol. I, pp. 421–422.

17. Within the homilies, the nature and evaluation of the scene of the Revelation at Sinai often change from one discussion to another, depending upon the specific contrast expressed.

18. *Kedushat Levi ha-shalem, Kedushah ḥamishit,* p. 390.

19. Ibid., p. 404, *Kelalot ha-nissim.*

20. Ibid., p. 102, Va-era.

21. Ibid., pp. 338–339, *Kedushah rishonah.*

22. Ibid., p. 213, *le-Shavuot.*

23. Ibid., p. 338, Pinḥas.

24. Ibid., p. 222, Shelaḥ-Lekha.

Seeing a Woman's
Beautiful Clothing

~

Among those who view a woman's beautiful garments, one whose thoughts are always directed toward women, God forbid, will not focus upon the embroidery and the gold in the clothing but instead his heart will immediately feel an attraction toward the woman who is wearing the garments. But another person, whose heart is pure, free of this desire, simply sees the article of clothing. Both of them look at the same thing, yet each sees something different.

And though removed a thousand times in terms of holiness and purity and impurity, in all that he sees in the world, the person who always longs for God, may He be blessed, beholds God whose powers sustain that which he sees, as it is written, "And You give life to them all" (Neh. 9:6). In contrast, the person lacking a strong desire for God in his thoughts sees only the material phenomena. And though if someone were to remind or ask him, he too would say that God gives life and being to everything, nonetheless he is not attached to that thought. *(Yosher divre emet)* [1]

The contrasting thrust of *mashal* and *nimshal*—a key element in the art of parable—is clearly evident in the above example from a text by Meshullam Feibush Heller of Zbarazh. What the *mashal* severely denigrates as carnal and sinful becomes, in the *nimshal*, analogous to a spiritual relationship to God. The story text reflects a rather conventional and accepted modesty (*tzeni'ut*), an attitude toward sexuality that takes clear precautions against any possibility of illicit desires. It condemns the person whose thoughts extend beyond the woman's ornate articles of clothing to the woman herself who is clad in them and to her body.[2]

The *nimshal*, however, discovers a metaphysical model precisely in that same person who cannot see the woman's clothing without thinking immediately of the woman herself who is wearing the garments. For the totality of the world can be likened to a garment in which the divine soul force and spiritual vitality (*hiyyut*) is clad. All the cosmos is as a garment (*malbush*) of God, and the universe conceals the Divine even as it also reveals something of that divine, spiritual presence that underlies physical being.

This parable exemplifies a significant strain of hasidic thought and of older kabbalistic teaching that perceives in erotic longing an intimation and analogy of longing for the Divine.[3] The hasidic ideal of *devekut*—a constant and deep inner attachment to God and an awareness of the presence of the Divine within and beyond all that exists—is likened to the love of a woman and to the physical expressions of that love.

The hasidic attraction to the biblical Song of Songs (*Shir ha-shirim*, which is, on the most obvious level, a collection of love poems) exemplifies that path of erotic longing as an intimation of longing for God. In his homiletic commentary on Song of Songs, Pinhas of Korets, a member of the Baal Shem Tov's circle, though in reality more a peer than a follower of the Besht, explains the utter impossibility of our comprehending that biblical text: "The entire Torah is a kind of averaging between the lowly world and the higher worlds, while the Song of Songs is an averaging between the higher worlds and [the even higher state of] divine infinitude. Furthermore, all the Prophets raised the lower world upward to the higher worlds, whereas the Song of Songs elevated those higher worlds upward to the level of *Ein Sof* [the infinite state of the Godhead] itself."[4]

1. *Yosher divre emet* (1974), #12, 7b.

2. Hasidic teaching often understands earthly erotic passion, especially improper feelings of love, as a fallen Holy Spark, in this case as a displacement of a higher love of God; and the person experiencing such passions is called upon to raise that desire to its higher form and reroot it in the world of the holy.

3. See "From the Sensuous to God," in Aryeh Wineman, *Beyond Appearances,* pp. 65–66, a translation of a story found in *Reshit hokhmah* (*Sha'ar ha-ahavah,* end of chap. 4) by Moshe ben Eliyahu deVadish. Along with the story, which is brought in the name of Yitzhak ben Shmuel of Acre and which can be seen to come from an Arabic source, the author of *Reshit hokhmah* quotes Yitzhak of Acre's conception, also found in Sufi texts, which views the love of a woman as a necessary model for the contemplation of God (Fenton, pp. 63–64).

4. *Likkute shoshanim* (1924), #83, p. 7a.

DEEPENING
THE
IMPLICATIONS
OF
DIVINE ONENESS

The Barriers to the Palace

～

king constructed a network of barriers on the way leading to his palace so that none might enter there; he hid in the palace while placing walls and fire and rivers—all of them illusions—on the way leading to the palace entrance.

The wise person, pondering what he sees, asks himself how it is possible that his merciful father would wish to hide from his beloved children. All this must indeed be a mere illusion, and the father is testing his son to ascertain whether he will make the effort to come to him. Immediately as the son plunges himself into the river surrounding the palace, the illusion vanishes and he proceeds onward through all the other barriers until he arrives at the king's palace. However, a fool, fearful of high walls and fire, would instead turn around and return home. (*Degel mahane Efrayim*)[1]

Rabbi Moshe Hayyim Efrayim of Sedilikov related this parable in connection with the verse, "I will keep my countenance hidden on that day . . ." (Deut. 31:18). The parable is found in a homily, included in *Degel mahane Efrayim*, in which Efrayim of Sedilikov wrestled with the logic and fairness of God's concealing His Presence from man. In Efrayim's own resolution of that question of the justice of God's hidden-ness, he suggested that through the consequent need to seek, the wise person ends up on a level higher than his prior spiritual level, and in this way the concealment of God's Presence is, paradoxically, for the benefit of the person's own spiritual development. The fool, who fails to pierce the illusion of divine concealment, fails to grow in stature, but a person of understanding grows as he moves from his initial sense of God's concealment to a sense of the Divine Presence within all existence, and he grasps that the cosmos itself is, in reality, a garment of the Divine.

The same parable, with slight variations, is found in a number of other early hasidic texts. Perhaps the clearest statement of the *nimshal* is that found following a version of the same parable as related by Rabbi Ya'akov Yosef of Polonnoye:

> The great King, the King of Kings, conceals Himself within numerous barriers and walls of iron; . . . the barriers are "extraneous thoughts" along with all that causes neglect of Torah study and prayer. . . . People of understanding realize that all the barriers and iron walls and all the garments and coverings are of His own self and being, as there is nothing devoid of His presence. . . . *(Beit porat Yosef)* [2]

The parable concerns all that people might experience as barriers to God, including those barriers that Jews encounter within themselves. These include an inability to pray because of extraneous thoughts (*mahshavot zarot*) that disturb one precisely when seeking to become attached to God in prayer. These barriers are indeed experienced as real and as frustrating. By means of the parable, however, the reader considers the possibility that God's Presence is everywhere, even behind all the barriers concealing the Divine, and even within a person's undesirable, disturbing thought, which nonetheless contains at its core a concealed and fallen Holy Spark.

Since ultimately there is only God—a fundamental principle of classical hasidic thought—the Divine is necessarily present within everything, including what appear to be barriers between man and God. These barriers, like everything else, lack any intrinsic being. Since there is no place and no substance devoid of God, it follows that the Divine is concealed within all that is, that the entire physical world is but a mask of God. That mask, it follows, implies the task and the test inherent in the human situation: to discover the Divine Presence concealed within all physical and psychological reality. As Efrayim of Sedilikov explains, the concealment comes, paradoxically, for the purpose of quest and of disclosure.

In the parable, barriers are placed on the way to the palace's entrance seemingly to deter and discourage the person seeking to enter the palace. In what follows, however, it becomes evident that the true intent is for the person to understand and acquire a perspective of the barriers and make the effort to enter. On the level of the *nimshal,* entering the palace is not a physical act but an inner state—a realization that ultimately only God is and that there is no place, no object, no moment, no state of being, and (perhaps above all) no thought in which God is not present. Hence the pilgrim journeying to the palace, confronting doubts and discouragement, is advised to ponder the paradoxical nature of all the barriers, of all that disturbs him, on his spiritual journey. As Efrayim of Sedilikov suggests, the experience of God's "hiding His face" appears to aggravate one's situation, but a person's consequent spiritual struggle and persistence contributes to raising the person toward a higher spiritual plane.

The parable includes a polarity of responses, those respectively of the fool and of the wise man, a polarity recognizable in many folktales and parables. The fool's response can be identified with what people presumably accept as a "common sense" view of the world, one assuming the reality of all such barriers. In contrast, the response of the wise person brings the listener to consider both the external reality about him and his own psychological makeup in a radically different light.

Within all that serves as a hurdle in the way of serving God, God is; within all one's doubts, God is present!

---

1. *Degel mahane Efrayim* (1963), pp. 264–265, Va-yelekh.
2. *Beit porat Yosef* (1884), *Derush le-shabbat ha-gadol,* 111a.

The King's Two Messengers

soldier appearing to summon a person to the king comes with great anger, evoking fear. His very garments inspire fear, and the person is indeed afraid of him. In truth, however, there is no reason to fear this messenger. His clothing is but a sign of his royal service, and in his own right he is nothing; the fear that he incites is the fear and the awe of the king. A wise person will have no fear of the messenger or of speaking to him but will instead simply proceed in haste to the king.

Or, it sometimes happens that a messenger from the king behaves in a very friendly way. A fool takes pleasure in the messenger and responds to his friendly words. The wise person, in contrast, knows that what is essential is the king's will itself, and so he thinks, "Why should I delay by conversing and taking delight in the messenger? Rather, I will proceed at once to the essential matter, to the real source of friendship and love." And so he goes directly to the king without giving any thought to the messenger. *(Maggid devarav le-Ya'akov)*[1]

The Maggid, Dov Baer of Mezherich, who related the above parable, provided for it the following explanation:

In this manner, whatever emotions come to a person in life, whether they are expressions of love or fear, that person will go to the King, the Holy One, blessed be He, and will elevate all [his emotions] to a higher plane. Whether he experiences an emotion of fear or injury, or of joy and delight, he will elevate both fear and love upward to the King on high; unlike the fool who delights in, and plays with, and eats, drinks, and spends time with the messenger whom the King has sent to him. . . .[2]

During the course of life, a person experiences both love and fear in various forms, along with other emotions. The words of the Maggid warn against becoming preoccupied with one's emotions, of whatever type they may be, for our emotions are really Divine Thoughts, Divine Letters that have become displaced, fallen from their proper station. They exemplify the fallen Holy Sparks of the Lurianic teaching, and one should immediately endeavor to raise those displaced letters to their higher source, to a higher level of love and fear in which those qualities are directed to God.

On a broader plane, one's fortunes or misfortunes in life are thought to be of no significance because all of life's events are, at their core, occasions of God's calling to humankind. To think otherwise is to deny the hasidic vision of Divine Oneness in which self is denied any reality separate from God.

The fool in the parable attaches importance to what he experiences in life. The presumption of the fool, in this case, is so generally accepted, so basic and pervasive in life, that an abstract statement posing an alternative way of thinking would be powerless to address the reader. For this reason, an alternative perspective is able to present itself and challenge the reader only by means of a parable, which turns that conventional, "commonsense" view on its head and allows one to consider a surprisingly different view of life. That alternative frame of reference completely transcends the World of Contraction—our lower level of reality in which our emotions appear to have significance in themselves.

The figure of the wise person in this parable represents a transcendent perspective. Neither fear (*yirah*), including displeasure and all that brings distress and insecurity, nor love (*ahavah*), including one's good fortune and happiness in life, is important in its own right. Rather, life's happenings, like our emotions, should be regarded as ways in which God addresses a person with the purpose of awakening him spiritually.[3] With this realization one's focus is removed from the immediate causes of either distress or happiness and is placed, instead, upon God who so addresses a person through all that happens to him in life. This realization shatters the expected and normative egocentricity of a person who is focused so heavily on the particular vicissitudes of life.

Precisely what a person normally considers of central importance, namely how life treats that person, is deemed irrelevant. What is relevant is his turning to engage in the service of God as a response to his lot in life, whatever it may be.[4]

---

1. *Maggid devarav le-Ya'akov* (1976), #161, pp. 261–262. Also found in *Likkutim yekarim* (1974), #98.
2. This *nimshal* is found in both of the above-mentioned texts.
3. *Maggid devarav le-Ya'akov,* #161, p. 258.
4. Ibid., p. 261.

On Evil as a Divine Instrument

∽

A king ruled over many lands near and far, and after a considerable period of time he wished to test the faithfulness of the inhabitants of those lands. He sent one of his servants, giving him different garments and having him speak in a different language as though he were a foreign king seeking to combat the true, legitimate king. Among the people of the land, some were prepared to fight against the apparent usurper, while others claimed, "We have no reason to fight him, and if he will be king we will accept him and serve him."

In time he came to one province where truly wise people lived and they pondered the matter from several different respects and inquired, "How is it possible that all this is as it seems on the surface? For it stands to reason that this man must be an agent whom the king sent to test the people's loyalty and ascertain whether they would rebel against the king." They then approached him and shared their thoughts with him, and he was satisfied and departed on his way. *(Toledot Ya'akov Yosef)* [1]

The opening of this parable is somewhat reminiscent of numerous folktales in which one person tests another or, more specifically, in which a ruler tests his subjects. The above parable, however, changes course from the familiar and expected pattern to exemplify a paradoxical viewpoint concerning evil.

Citing a similar parable found in the Zohar,[2] Rabbi Ya'akov Yosef of Polonnoye explained in connection with his own parable that while the Evil Inclination (yetzer ha-ra) found within each person would seem to be a force in opposition to God, in truth it is an agent of God commissioned to entice and test the person. The agent's change of garb and speech in the parable suggests that the force encouraging or inciting rebellion is, in reality, but a disguise. A monistic and acosmic faith that views God as the sole true reality and views all of existence as a garment of the Divine leaves no room for a counterforce. It also negates the sense of mythic conflict inherent in much of kabbalistic thought, from the Zohar through Lurianic Kabbalah and its later expressions. What would seem to be a force in opposition to God—a negative and arrogant impulse within the human makeup countering the Divine—is in truth nothing other than a disguise of the Divine. And immediately with the moment of realization when the wise person sees through that disguise, the Evil Inclination is left powerless.

Ya'akov Yosef added in the name of his teacher, the Baal Shem Tov, that "in every distress, material or spiritual, when the person realizes that even in that distress God is present though in disguise, the garb is then removed and the distress annulled, this being the case also concerning evil decrees."[3] Ya'akov Yosef's comment provides a very different dimension to the parable's meaning as distress assumes the place of the Evil Inclination. One might perhaps understand his comment as suggesting that with a realization of God's clandestine presence even within distress, one no longer experiences the distress in the same way. That very realization is itself redemptive, and distress loses its total domination over the person.

Another version of this parable found elsewhere in the same text[4] mentions the great efforts and precautions to which some of the provinces go to defend themselves against the presumed rebel. Viewed in perspective, these efforts are superfluous and irrelevant. That alteration of the mashal voices a protest against one's relating to the Evil Inclination as an enemy and against a person's consequent engaging in involved strategies designed to protect oneself against one's own Evil Inclination. What is required instead is simply to grasp that the Evil Inclination is but a disguise, having no independent reality in itself. More specifically, the author of the *Toledot* stresses that it is unnecessary to combat the Evil Inclination with ascetic afflictions of the flesh,[5] for with the realization that it is acting merely as an agent of God, it is possible "to conquer the Evil Inclination without war."[6]

---

1. *Toledot Ya'akov Yosef* (1973), Bereshit, 1:25.
2. Zohar 2:163a. In that parable, a king invites a prostitute to the palace to entice his son so that the king might be able to test his son's moral behavior and willpower.
3. *Toledot Ya'akov Yosef,* op. cit.
4. Ibid., Va-yakhel, 1:252; also Va-era, 1:60.
5. Ascetic practices were largely influenced by Lurianic Kabbalah and its offshoots.
6. *Toledot Ya'akov Yosef,* Va-yakhel, 1:252.

On Intruding Thoughts

hen a person is standing in the presence of the king and speaking with him, it would certainly be improper and impudent for any of the king's servants to call out to that person and to chat with him, interrupting that person's meeting with the king for matters lacking any import. For without any doubt, a servant who would interrupt the king's meeting with that person would be guilty of a highly serious, even grave, transgression. And should one of the king's servants call to a person and converse with him, it stands to reason that he is acting in accordance with a directive from the king himself.

[Or] it may be that the servant is announcing that he too is in need of the king but is unable to approach the king while clad in his garment of sackcloth, and so he requests of that person having an audience with the king to have him in his thoughts and remove the servant's sackcloth, clothing him instead in respectable and beautiful garments so that he, too, may be able to come before the king. . . . *(Degel maḥane Efrayim)*[1]

Building upon the foundation of kabbalistic thought, Hasidism deepened the meaning of monotheism to negate not only other divine powers but to deny any existence separate from and independent of God. Accordingly, faith in the One who is the Creator and Master of all, according to Moshe Hayyim Efrayim of Sedilikov, implies that when an extraneous thought (*maḥshavah zarah*) comes to one's mind during prayer, the person should not cease or interrupt his praying. His continuing to pray at such a time affirms that the "strange thought" came to him for the specific purpose that he repair that thought so that it might be able to ascend to its real Root in the holy.

Such an extraneous thought might be disturbing or embarrassing or distasteful, and it tends to enter a person's mind especially while that person seeks to focus solely on his prayer with true and complete concentration. In this particular homily, Efrayim of Sedilikov emphasized that the particular thought does not come to that person simply by chance. For every thought, even such a disturbing thought, is a kind of garment in which is clad a Holy Spark of the Divine. The Holy Spark, however, is in a fallen state, and it comes to a person who is capable of redeeming it not by dispelling or suppressing it, but rather by elevating the evil thought to its higher, holy Root. For every thought, in its proper and true state, is holy; only in its present degenerate form is the thought in exile. The person to whom the thought comes has the task of seeking and focusing upon the pure and holy core of the evil thought that comes to him. In this way he transforms its character and elevates it to its true, higher nature.

In the fallen state in which it comes to a person, the thought is unable to return to its higher Root just as, in the parable, the king's servant, while dressed in sackcloth (mourning clothes), is not permitted to enter the royal chamber to appear before the king. The image of mourning clothes in the parable evokes not disgust but rather pity and sympathy. In desperation, the unfortunate thought is calling to a particular person to help it. And in likening the disturbing thought to a royal servant, the parable elevates its character and moral status in the mind of the listener. While the reader might initially condemn the devotee for his thoughts, the simile provides a different lens through which to view such troublesome, extraneous thoughts. The exiled and soiled spark calls to a person and disturbs his audience with the King (his act of prayer and devotion), asking that person to focus upon the higher state of that extraneous thought.

In doing so the person removes its shameful sackcloth and it assumes a respectable garment in which it is restored to its higher, Divine Source and "appears before the King."

As all space and time are part of the greater Divine reality, so is every thought. Just as nothing ultimately exists other than God, so a thought, whether desirable or undesirable, is also an expression of the sole divine reality and is ultimately inseparable from God.

The problem of *mahshavot zarot* as a barrier in the life of prayer and devotion was an issue of grave importance in the background of the emergence of Hasidism.[2] The Baal Shem Tov is associated with a resolution of that barrier, namely to perceive the thought not as something to be expelled or shattered but rather to be elevated to a higher level.[3] The devotee does this by attaching himself to the higher aspect of the same thought beyond the husk in which it appears. The elevation of such foreign thoughts became a core concept in the teaching of the Maggid of Mezherich.

That concept, however, was not always considered to be available to the general following of Hasidism, and even in an early period was trusted only to those on the level of the spiritual elite.[4] It was feared that attaching oneself to the disturbing thought in any way might open the door to moral dangers. Over time it became clear that only the *tzaddik* (the holy man who came to serve as center of a hasidic community) was considered to be capable of satisfactorily engaging in that practice. The practice of *mahshavot zarot*, so significant in the earlier stages of Hasidism, lost its importance as it came to be considered beyond the legitimate realm of the *tzaddik's* followers, who were not on his level and were therefore generally encouraged to restrict their spiritual life to the more conventional aspects of religious living.[5]

---

1. *Degel mahane Efrayim* (1963), p. 235, Ekev.
2. Mendel Piekarz, *Bi-yeme tzemihat ha-hasidut* (1978), pp. 269–279.
3. *Shivhe ha-Besht* (1947), p. 82.
4. Mendel Piekarz, *Bi-yeme tzemihat ha-hasidut* (1978), pp. 275–276.
5. See Miles Krassen, *Uniter of Heaven and Earth,* pp. 208–213. See also Naftali Lowenthal, in Ada Rapoport-Albert, ed., *Hasidism Reappraised,* p. 280.

It Is God Who Awakens
Our Minds

⌒

A guest comes to the king to test the knowledge of the king's son, and the young child
is unable even to understand the halakhah[1]
because of its deep and complicated logic.
But because of the father's great affection for his son, he
can't bear the distress his beloved son experiences in
encountering such difficulty and in his incapability to
comprehend. What does the father do? He finds a way
to help his son begin to understand the halakhah and he
shows him a path that might allow him to converse on
that passage, virtually telling him the actual content of
that legal passage.

The guest poses questions, and when the young boy is
able to respond and engage in dialogue with a clarity of
thought, the father rejoices, feeling delight and pride in
his son, even though the latter's very ability to answer
and discuss the passage is admittedly the doing of his
father.

Cognizant of the father's delight, the guest goes on to
raise further questions, and relying on his father's prod-
ding, the son's understanding awakens and he proceeds
to answer the difficulties posed by the guest. . . .
(Or torah)[2]

The Maggid, Dov Baer of Mezherich, who told this parable, identified the guest who comes to probe the child's learning—and possibly
also to embarrass him if necessary—with the *yetzer ha-ra* (the Evil
Inclination), and in the Maggid's homily, the *mashal* is said to exemplify
an overcoming of that Evil Inclination. The guest, a person steeped in talmudic learning, occupies a role in the parable counter to that of the child,
and his role in testing echoes the traditional role of a Satan figure in testing people in many folktales. Though the Maggid was himself an
extremely capable talmudic scholar, that overtone suggests a critical attitude toward the learned class whose representatives, in the hasidic writings of that period, are often closely associated with pride. The parable
provides its own answer to pride in conveying that one's accomplish-
ments are not really one's own; even our own spiritual and intellectual
attainments are really not of our own doing but rather depend upon
God's awakening us, as the Maggid goes on to explain:

> We find that everything is of You and from You, and
> our own doing and endeavor is from You, of Your own
> power, and nevertheless You have great delight from
> this. And You feel pride in us as though we ourselves
> have really accomplished what we have done. And in
> this condition one can recognize the force of Your love
> and Your overflowing affection. *(Or torah)* [3]

As noted, The Maggid's homily explains the above parable in more precise terms as it applies to the righteous person's ability to overpower the
Evil Inclination (*yetzer ha-ra*). God takes great delight when such a person prevails over the Evil Inclination, over his own negative tendencies,
even though the very capacity to prevail over the evil within one's own
makeup is itself a gift from God, not something of one's own making.
Nevertheless, the Maggid emphasizes, God takes delight in man's suc-
cessful wrestling with evil as though the feat is really man's doing, independent of God.

1. The law or legal passage concerning which the child was being questioned.
2. *Or torah* (1910), on Ps. 48:2, pp. 79–80. The same basic parable is found also in *Likkutim yekarim* (1974), #266.
3. *Or torah,* p. 80.

Child and Parent

✒

I

A parable of a father whose child lacks nothing; within his home he has wealth and treasure. The father's delight is that he sees his child whenever he wishes, and the child—to whom God has given everything—delights and rejoices not in the goodness and blessing that have been given him, but rather solely in that he brings delight to his father.

Similarly, the *tzaddik* who serves the Lord with all his heart [with a wholeness and purity of motivation] takes delight neither in his serving God nor in the great goodness that is prepared for him in the time to come; rather his sole joy and delight is that through his service he brings delight to God. *(Kedushat Levi)*[1]

This seemingly very simple parable told by Rabbi Levi Yitzhak of Berdichev exemplifies a recurrent contrast in the teachings of the Berdichever between what might be designated as *thingness* and *personness*. Reward and consideration of reward are associated with the quality of *thingness*. They are marked by concern with what one can derive for oneself through a relationship with the other. *Personness*, in contrast, is indifferent to reward and personal advantage and casts the spotlight instead on the other person for the latter's own sake. In *personness*, the other person is an end in himself or herself rather than a means to enhancing one's own self.

94

As the reader might well expect, the parable is explained in reference to one's relationship with God. One's proper relationship with God is to exemplify the quality of *personness,* not *thingness.* God is not a tool or instrument for the purpose of bestowing blessing upon humankind.[2] To love or serve God because one expects to gain something by it is neither love nor true service.

Perhaps the most significant nuance overheard in this parable story is the choice of a child to exemplify a stance of *personness.* The very choice of a child image for that role would seem to imply that others, of greater worldly maturity, are incapable of the same unqualified and disinterested love. In apparent contrast with the motif—so frequently seen in the parables of the Maggid and the Berdichever and others—of the father or teacher who must contract his intelligence in order to teach or interact with a young child, in this parable the child, in his innocence, is able to understand innately what adults are unable to grasp. Adults are tainted by a distinct sense of ego and a focus on considerations of self. The adult more readily asks, "What's in it for me?" The adult world is morally complex; relationships are generally based on one's seeing oneself as the center of life and one's own needs as being of primary importance, unlike the radical innocence of the child portrayed in the above parable.

The *nimshal* speaks of the *tzaddik*[3] who parallels the role of the child in relation to God; his happiness—as for a child—is not in anything he himself experiences or expects as reward, but solely in his bringing delight to God. And yet there is presumably a decisive difference between the young child and the holy man. The *mashal* describes a child not yet tainted by ego. The adult cannot instinctively know that kind of radical innocence but must rather make the effort to overcome and negate his sense of self and to return, to the extent possible, to the lost but purer state symbolized by the child figure. As a mature human being, the *tzaddik* must also make the effort to bypass and negate the impact of self *(bitul atzmi),* an effort that in the hasidic complex of values is a central aspect of *avodah* (the worship and service of God).[4]

The general picture that emerges from the child image in this parable, as in modern child psychology, perceives early childhood as a stage preceding the development of self-awareness, which gradually distinguishes self from non-self. While psychology views that awareness as a necessary and indispensable stage in a person's acquiring a sense of identity, hasidic teaching perceives in that same sense of self the seed of ego and pride—the basic flaw in human character. The child in the parable serves as a mirror image of the difficult goal of *bitul atzmi*—the overcoming and unlearning of egoism on the part of the more mature person and awareness of oneself in the presence of God as a mere candle whose light is nullified by the brightness of a torch.[5]

Bitul atzmi, the psychological annihilation of self, is a precondition of *devekut*, the devotional ideal of Hasidism. Meshullam Feibush Heller of Zbarazh defined the state of true *devekut* (an intense and constant mental attachment to God), employing the analogies of a branch having a sense of complete oneness with the root so that it lacks any sense of its identity apart from the root or tree; and of "a drop of water that falls into the ocean becoming one with the ocean's water, no longer having a separate identity."[6]

Like the branch or the drop of water, and like the world itself, a person is not separable from God, and the thought that anything, especially the self, has any real existence apart from the Divine is considered a form of idolatry, perhaps the truest and ultimate idolatry. The parable's depiction of the young child's intuitive sense of things, devoid of ego, is a mirror of the deeper realization that ego is not only idolatry but also an illusion from which people must liberate themselves in order to realize the full implications of Divine Oneness.

A comment of the Maggid of Mezherich,[7] the Berdichever's teacher, considers the young son (the younger, the better) as "close to the supernal Will, meaning the *ayin* (nothingness)," the infinite or near infinite state of the Divine.[8] The young child is both endeared and idealized. He is closer, in his own character, to the *ayin*, which also represents one's own self-negation, emptying oneself of all egocentrism in order that in its place a deeper Divine energy (*hiyyut*) might be infused. The younger the child, the more he or she reflects that state of *ayin*, which precedes concrete, physical existence and which is incompatible with ego. At the opposite spectrum of the life cycle, one's acceptance of death is considered a moment of realizing the quality of *ayin* insofar as one becomes "like a loving son with his father even though [the latter] has not given him anything."[9]

II

A very young child pursues some very childish thing and his thoughts turn away from his father. But afterward, upon seeing his father, he casts everything aside out of his desire for him and thinks only of him, running to him, all because he is made of the very substance of his father. *(Yosher divre emet)*[10]

Two contradictory processes—two aspects of one comprehensive rhythm—are represented in this brief parable. At first the child forgets his father but later, when he catches sight of him, all of his thoughts turn completely toward his father.

In the analogy of this parable story, Meshullam Feibush Heller of Zbarazh explained the two contradictory impulses that he believed are inherent in humans. The very existence of the cosmos necessitates a distancing from the Divine, from the Root of all being, to allow for the existence of something other than the Divine in its totally infinite and unbounded state *(Ein Sof)*. That first impulse parallels the earlier kabbalistic concept of *tzimtzum* (contraction), a process of creating that space or vacuum that can allow for a cosmos to come into being. That first motion effects a necessary distance between existence itself and its Divine Root—between the world and God. In his attempt to dissect the text of the Torah according to the use of divine names, drawn in part from a much older kabbalistic text, *Ginat egoz*,[11] Meshullam Feibush, in this same homily, connects the name *Elohim* with the physical character of the created world, which intrinsically makes for separateness and distance.

The second impulse or motion in the analogy represents, in contrast, a coming near, a transcending of distance. After the initial phase of the emergence of a world outside God, as it were, the more inner aspect of Divinity, alluded to in the Tetragrammaton (the four-letter name of God), is revealed. This phase, in contrast with the former, is one of spirituality, of a drawing near to the Divine. The Tetragrammaton, representing the inner being and life of God, impacts created beings with a longing for their spiritual Root, a longing to become one with God and restore the seemingly lost state of Divine Oneness. Of the pair of divine names, the first suggests what is readily visible, while the second, in contrast, suggests what is hidden within all being.

In contrast with the previous parable of Levi Yitzhak of Berdichev, Meshullam Feibush, in his parable, notes the child's initial drawing away from his parent as well as his subsequent longing for his parent. Meshullam Feibush restates, in his parable, the belief of the Maggid and his students (mentioned above) that the coming into existence of a world requires a distancing, a forgetting of the Divine as a prerequisite for the existence of the non-Divine. But these same teachers add that God also wills a countercurrent in which one is drawn toward the Divine. For this purpose, Meshullam Feibush explaines, God gives the human being a glimpse of His own spiritual light, which evokes in that human a longing for God. It is that countercurrent, according to the homily, which is represented by the change in the use of divine names from *Elohim* to the Tetragrammaton.

Meshullam Feibush goes on to explain the word "Shabbat" as derived from the root *le-hashiv* (to restore). The Shabbat (the seventh day) turns the Jew toward God, a returning to the source of existence. The Shabbat comprises the second of the two processes involved in Creation. It connotes longing and a nearness that transcend the prior and necessary phase of distance between man and God and between the world and God. The nature of Shabbat is the longing to overcome one's seemingly separate and independent existence—a longing for a restored oneness with God.[12]

Upon catching sight of his father, the child in the parable feels a powerful longing for him because his parents are the very source of his existence. Even while physically separated from them, the child is still biologically, in a sense, part of his parents who brought him into being; he is formed of their substance.

On the level of the *nimshal*, our source is God. The deepest levels of the human soul are formed within the divine realm and the human being is, in this sense, "a portion of the supernal God." Not only is God the source of our existence, but each person is, in some significant sense, a part of the Divine—just as biologically and physically each child remains part of his or her parents. Classical hasidic thought would define one's awareness of a connection with the Divine Root as the very nature of spirituality. In the nature of things, such spirituality must follow a prior focus upon the physical and upon separateness, upon the ultimately illusionary sense of the world and of oneself as being realities in themselves, separate from the Divine, which is hidden within all that exists. The child's intuitive sense of things, devoid of ego, provides a clearer sense of reality, for in his own simple and unsophisticated way, he mirrors the deeper realization that ego is illusion.

That twofold rhythm can be overheard in various spiritual myths and in the teachings of various thinkers. For example, it can be identified in the writings of Aharon David Gordon, the thinker and sage who came to the land of Israel as a pioneer during the early years of the twentieth century. The overcoming of the illusion of independence and separateness occupies a central place in the thought of Gordon, who was influenced by Jewish mystic thought. With the development of a sense of self—which goes hand in hand with the emergence of cognitive thinking over against immediate intuitive experience—human beings, Gordon maintained, forego a relationship of integral belonging and connection with the totality of life and being, and through that with God. And that very sense of self gives rise to a painful state of alienation from the cosmos as a whole. This disconnection, according to Gordon, is represented in the biblical account of man and woman's eating of the fruit of the Tree of Knowledge and their consequent expulsion from the Garden of Eden. The essence of religion in its broadest sense, according to Gordon, is the human groping to heal one's sense of ego and separateness so that individually and collectively, one may transcend his nature as a "knowing being" and again feel himself an inseparable part of the totality of being. Gordon's viewpoint echoes some of the insights of kabbalistic and hasidic teaching and comprises one of many variations on this aspect of hasidic thought.[13]

1. *Kedushat Levi ha-shalem* (1993), p. 178, Shemini. There is some confusion between the levels of *mashal* and *nimshal* in the wording of the parallel, and the reader will probably conclude that in the actual parable story it is the child's father, rather than God, who has given him "goodness and blessing."

2. The Berdichever accentuates this theme, even considering the concept of *shefa* (abundance), the flow of divine energy, which manifests itself both materially and spiritually. The latter is emphasized in Moshe Idel's *Hasidism.*

3. The holy man and central figure in a hasidic community.

4. The tendency to annihilate one's sense of self finds parallels and expressions in the mystic expression of other religious traditions. The medieval Christian text *The Cloud of Unknowing*, for example, speaks about the absolute need to rid oneself of all sense of one's own existence as a prerequisite for true contemplation (*The Cloud of Unknowing*, chap. 43; Karen Armstrong, ed., *Visions of God*, pp. 96–98).

5. Based on the talmudic saying (B. Pesaḥim 8a), "To what are the righteous *[tzaddikim]* likened when adjacent to the Divine Presence? To a candle in the presence of a torch."

6. *Yosher divre emet* (1974), #14, 9b. Moshe Idel (in *Hasidism*, pp. 108–109) makes the point that the negation of self is not of the nature of annihilation of self but rather of an expansion of consciousness, the emptying of ego allowing for an infusion of spiritual power from a higher reality. The devotee's attaining a state of *ayin* makes his new state analogous to the highest plane of the Divine.

7. *Maggid devarav le-Ya'akov* (1976), #178.

8. See Daniel Matt, *"Ayin: The Concept of Nothingness in Jewish Mysticism."*

9. *Likkutim yekarim* (1974), #193.

10. *Yosher divre emet* (1974), #46, 29b.

11. Written by Yosef Gikatilla, 1274.

12. See Miles Krassen, *Uniter of Heaven and Earth*, pp. 147–161, "The Sacred Calendar and Devequt."

13. See Samuel Hugo Bergman, *Faith and Reason: Modern Jewish Thought*, pp. 98–120. Also note Eli Schweid, *Ha-Yaḥid;* and Avraham Shapiro, *Or ha-ḥayyim be-yom ketanot. Mishnat A.D. Gordon u-mekoroteha be-kabbalah uve-ḥasidut.*

The Ultimate Disloyalty

 parable of a king who gives substantial wages to his servant that he might carry out his wishes whenever the king might require his service. . . . And the servant takes those wages and goes instead to carry out the wishes of another king who is hostile to the servant's own king and employer. Now, could there be a greater act of rebellion and disloyalty than this? Indeed, he would deserve death at the hands of his king.

And the *nimshal:* This is what happens when one takes the divine life force that belongs to the King of Kings, the Holy One, blessed be He, the sole purpose of which is to enable a person to do the Divine Will, and rebels, using it instead to do the will of the *sitra ah'ra*[1] and the *kelipah,*[2] which the King of Kings, the Holy One, blessed be He, detests. *(Sod ehad dekri'at shema)*[3]

Hasidic teaching emphasizes that apart from *hiyyut* (the divine life force activating all that is),[4] nothing whatsoever could exist. And it is that same life force—Divine in origin and nature—that accounts for whatever capacities we have, including the ability to see and hear, speak and think, etc. The concept of *hiyyut* implies also that our perceptions of multiplicity, along with those of separateness and separate identity, are ultimately inaccurate. The *hiyyut,* which participates in any person and any existing entity, is also the same sole divine life force that enables the existence of all that is.

David of Malke'iv in Podolia, evidently a contemporary of the Baal Shem Tov,[5] explained paradoxically that even the pleasure one derives from a transgression would not be possible apart from that *hiyyut,* the purpose of which is to enable man to serve God. People commit evil acts on the premise that they are masters of their own energies and capacities, of their own life and being. But in committing a transgression, one is actually employing what is God's in order to serve the *sitra aḥ'ra* and the *kelipah,* which, according to the kabbalistic worldview, will one day be annulled in favor of an unmarred wholeness and holiness throughout all existence.

The reader who views his whole life experience in the light of this parable will grasp its message: if that life force is Divine, then its purpose is to bring us to serve God, pursue Torah and mitzvot, and cleave to the Divine Root of our existence and of all existence. It follows that when we employ the capacities we have—along with our very gift of life—not for the service of God, but rather for evil and selfish purposes, that is nothing less than an act of theft. It is the ultimate expression of betrayal against the very source of our being.

---

1. "The Other Side," the unholy and impure reality, the antithesis of the Divine. According to kabbalistic thought, the *sitra aḥ'ra* emerged largely as a by-product of the processes and crises of divine emanation.
2. "Shell," the depth of darkness comprising the lowest levels of being; in Lurianic teaching, the containers of the Divine Light that failed to contain that Light and fell to the depths when those containers were themselves shattered.
3. From comments added to the printing of *Sod eḥad dekri'at shema* by Rabbi David of Malke'iv; included in the volume, *Ḥesed le-Avraham /mashmi'a shalom,* p. 96.
4. From the root meaning "life," the term is possibly based on the biblical verse, "You keep them all alive," (Neh. 9:6).
5. Malke'iv was located in Podolia. David of Malke'iv is possibly the person mentioned in a legend in *Shivḥe ha-Besht,* the classic collections of legends about the Baal Shem Tov, which appeared in 1815. See Aryeh Rubenstein, *Shivḥe ha-Besht* (1991), p. 79.

Transforming Sadness
from Within

⌐⌐

Sometimes when people are rejoicing and dancing in a circle, and there is a man outside the circle who is immersed in sadness and depression, they will grab him and bring him into the dance against his will and force him to rejoice with them.

Gladness and joy should pursue and grab sadness and sighing, which flee from the very presence of joy, in order to bring them within the orbit of joy even against their will. For there is that sadness and sighing that are really the *sitra aḥ'ra*[1] and that have no desire to be a foundation[2] for the holy, and so they flee from the very presence of joy. Therefore it is necessary to force them into the realm of the holy and its joy, against their own will. (*Likkute Moharan tinyana*)[3]

Joy—it is often maintained in hasidic literature—brings one closer to God, while sadness and depression distance a person from God. The hasidic attitude toward joy and sadness convey in their way some rather obvious psychological insights, namely that sadness, often bound up with guilt, is also associated with a preoccupation with self, whereas joy opens the human heart to go beyond such preoccupation with self in favor of a broader focus.

Rabbi Nahman distinguished between *lev nishbar* (a broken heart, flowing from regret and remorse) and *marah sheḥorah* (a prevailing and

ongoing sadness bordering upon and extending to depression).[4] The former is itself positive in nature, but such contemplation of regret should
be limited in time to an hour a day, with the rest of the day given over to
joy. He taught that "it is a great mitzvah[5] always to be joyous,"[6] and he
also diagnosed physical illnesses as flowing from a depressive spirit,
whereas he considered joy to be a cure for illness. He approved even of
saying foolish words if they can be instrumental in helping a person to
experience joy.[7]

In the above parable and its explanation, Rabbi Nahman suggests that
the correct way to overcome sadness and depression is not to seek to dis-
pel or fight them; doing so is often a fruitless endeavor. It is rather to deal
with the sadness and depression at their root, transforming the depression into joy and bringing the sadness into the circle of joy. In the parable, when the person afflicted with sadness makes a connection through
his joining in the circle—even involuntarily—he opens within himself a
space for joy. An inner as well as an external connection occurs. The inner
connection is a reconnection with God and with a human community—
an act of turning (teshuvah) with a realization that the Divine is clad even
within the depression (marah shehorah) itself. That realization conquers
the depression from within and transforms it into joy.

A pronounced effort is required to transform sadness and depression
into joy, for the former states can offer strong and determined resistance
against defeat at the hands of joy. In his conceptual frame of reference
based upon kabbalistic teaching, Rabbi Nahman associates those negative
emotional states with the sitra ah'ra; demonic in nature, they forcibly
resist joy. Ultimately, however, even that impure character of sadness can
be transformed, for the holy, equated with joy, is present even within
sadness.

The nimshal conveys that the person standing outside the circle—the
person so immersed in sadness and depression—is sadness personified,
whereas those dancing in the circle represent the quality of simhah (joy).
Joy must capture and convert sadness, making it part of joy itself.

As manifestations of the sitra ah'ra, sadness and depression are a denial
of God's Oneness and they function counter to the Divine. Conversely,
their being grabbed into the circle of dancers represents a realization of
Divine Oneness, annulling the expression of that counterforce within life
and within the cosmos.

1. A kabbalistic term indicating the evil, impure, demonic reality that emerged within the course of the primordial cosmic kabbalistic processes and that counters the holy.
2. Literally, "chariot."
3. *Likkute Moharan tinyana, #23.*
4. *Sihot Haran, #41.*
5. Commanded deed, or holy act.
6. *Likkute Moharan tinyana, #24.*
7. Ibid.

ECHOES
AND
TRANSFORMATIONS
OF
OLDER MOTIFS*

∽

*This section, in slightly different form, originally appeared in my article "Wedding-Feasts, Exiled Princes, and Hasidic Parable-Traditions," in *Hebrew Studies,* Vol. 40 (1999), pp.191–216, and appears here with the permission of the editor.

The World Is like a
Wedding Feast:
A Parable Tradition

⌒

hen people come to a wedding, one person rejoices in the food he eats—in fish and meat and the like—while another rejoices in the music played on instruments, while still others find joy in other things. And there are those like the parents who do not turn their attention at all to the food and drink but who rejoice in the wedding itself. But no one can rejoice in all the various joys together. And even that person who rejoices in all these various things does not experience joy in all of them at the same time, but rather one at a time, consecutively. . . . But the wholeness of joy is known only by the person able to rejoice in all these goods together, simultaneously. (*Likkute Moharan tinyana*)[1]

Rabbi Nahman of Bratslav, who related this parable, went on to explain that "only the person who looks above all the good things and considers the Root from which all the various goods are drawn" is able to rejoice in all the goods at the very same time. That is true because "there, at the Root, all is one." That higher Source transcends the divisions and differentiation and the utter variety of phenomena, sensations, and emotions that mark our own human level of experience. And among the examples of guests at a wedding and their diverse foci, there is one among them, presumably a holy man—a *tzaddik* (presumably Rabbi Nahman

109

himself)—who fully attains a transcendental vision of the Divine Source of all that exists.

The Bratslaver was not alone in employing the image of a wedding festivity in a parable. One notes the same image, for example, in a parable related by Rabbi Levi Yitzhak of Berdichev in connection with a talmudic saying, "*olma damya le-hilula*" (the world is likened to a wedding feast).[2]

When one makes a wedding festivity for his son or daughter, he gathers all the townspeople and people of the surrounding area for a feast, preparing for them big meals with rich dishes and sweet drinks. Now, does it make sense for him to give his bread to strangers and to pour wine for them? Is the wedding not his own joyous event? And so wouldn't it be more fitting for him to eat and drink and rejoice without having strangers present at his joyous celebration? But [he does it because] the joy of the occasion is increased and enhanced through a joyous event with many invited guests. The host of the occasion, however, is busy all the days of the feast, working ceaselessly without rest, each day preparing all kinds of tasty dishes for the guests. And when will the host himself be able to rejoice? For it is most appropriate for him to rejoice, as the guests are present solely for the purpose of augmenting his own joy.

And so after all the guests have left and gone home, the wise host will sit down with the members of his own family joyously to eat and drink, and for this purpose he sets aside a good serving for himself and his family.

The foolish host, in contrast, gives no thought to putting aside a good serving for himself, and so when the guests consume everything, nothing remains for him. When the noise and excitement have quieted down and

all the guests have gone home, nothing at all remains
with which he himself might rejoice. *(Kedushat Levi)*[3]

The Berdichever goes on to explain the *nimshal* as follows:

It is true that one requires the needs of this world in
order to engage in serving the Creator, for it is impossible to serve [God] while one lacks clothing and food
and drink and life's other essentials. But at the same
time, all those are secondary, the central thing being a
person's service to his Creator. For therein lies the true
joy of his soul and its sustenance and delight after the
noise and excitement of the afflicted body has quieted,
and the soul enters into the world of souls.

The *mashal* taken by itself offers what would appear to be some very
practical advice, without anything particularly ennobling about it. The
nimshal, however, comprises an emphatic turn in a new and unexpected
direction. The bringing together of the two parts of the parable, each having a very different character, is a key to the parable's literary power.
When the model of the parable is placed over the *nimshal,* the strangers
(the invited guests) are identified as a person's worldly needs. The parable
abruptly shatters the orientation of those for whom the satisfaction of
worldly, physical needs occupies center stage. Those needs now appear
instead as foreign to one's real self, which is identified with the soul and
which has its own needs. The motif of the wedding feast is made to convey the spiritual tragedy of overlooking one's true, spiritual needs.

Let us look at another example of a hasidic parable that projects the
image of a wedding festivity, this time a parable told by Moshe Hayyim
Efrayim of Sedilikov. Relating to a verse from the Torah that introduces
the instructions for the building of the Tabernacle during the period of
the wandering in the wilderness, Efrayim of Sedilikov focuses upon the
word *li* (to me or for me) in Exodus 25:2 ("Tell the Israelites to bring Me
gifts. . . .").

The whole wedding and all its preparations are for the sole purpose of bringing joy to the bridegroom and the bride. There are people, however, who focus upon what is really secondary, and so they come only to eat and drink and ignore the essential matter.

And similarly, this world is likened to a wedding celebration, and all that the Holy One, blessed be He, created in His world is for the intended purpose of "uniting bride and groom." But there are many people who wish only to eat and drink and pursue pleasures, and they ignore the central purpose of the whole matter. But the wise and understanding person strives solely to unite the Bridegroom and the Bride, the unification of the Holy One, blessed be He, and the Shekhinah, and ignores all the delights of this world. *(Degel mahane Efrayim)*[4]

While referring to that same talmudic saying—likening the world to a wedding feast—the focus in this parable is on God and divine needs. All of our life and efforts in this world are to be directed toward effecting a restored oneness within the higher worlds, within the divine substratum of our own plane of experience and of all existence, and that oneness is symbolized, in the parable, by the image of the wedding and the union of bride and groom. In reference to this parable, Efrayim of Sedilikov goes on to explain that the Israelite, in contributing material for the Tabernacle, was to remove himself from what is purely secondary and to grasp the essential: that need for cosmic and divine union and unification.

Still another parable having to do with a wedding festivity is found in a homily by Rabbi Ya'akov Yosef of Polonnoye. His parable, too, comes in connection with the Torah account of the building of the Tabernacle. In that context, Ya'akov Yosef quotes an interpretation by the *maggid*, Menahem Mendel, of that same talmudic saying that likens the world to a wedding feast.

How much trouble and effort and energy go into a wedding celebration, while the real purpose of the entire celebration is the word *li* [to me; referring to the bridegroom's declaration to his betrothed, *harei at mekudeshet li*. . . . "Behold you are betrothed to me with this ring. . . ."], signifying that the bridegroom hallows [*kadesh*, "sets apart"] this woman [from all others], as his bride. Actually, all the things of this world have a similar purpose—that [through them] one might be able to hallow [*kadesh*] oneself to cleave to [God], may He be blessed, the purpose suggested in the word *li* [to Me]. (*Toledot Ya'akov Yosef*)[5]

That little word *li*, found in the traditional Jewish marriage declaration, occurs also, as noted above in the parable by Efrayim of Sedilikov, in reference to contributions for the Tabernacle. Just as a ring or other gift is given to the bride to signify the establishment of a hallowed relationship with her, so also, Rabbi Ya'akov Yosef of Polonnoye explains, by extension, is it that the true purpose of all the things of this world and of all one's endeavors in the world is to allow for a person's inner attachment to God. But just as people can lose sight of the real purpose of a wedding celebration, so can they similarly lose sight of the meaning of human life. When that happens, we tend to regard the things of this world as ends in themselves instead of utilizing the gifts and resources of life for the purpose of entering into a holy relationship with the Divine.

These parables, which employ the analogy of the wedding celebration, comprise a rather unusual kind of subgenre of the hasidic parable; unusual because such an example of parables by different masters on a specific talmudic saying is not common. Each of the above parables has interpreted, in its own particular direction, that analogy of the world to a wedding festivity, an analogy which in the talmudic source is less than edifying as it conveys the counsel to hurry and consume one's share of the world before we must leave it and the feast, for us, is over!

Two of the above four parables relate explicitly, in their homiletic context, to the portions of the Torah devoted to the Tabernacle—a detail inviting analysis. And in light of various associations of the Tabernacle in earlier sources, it would appear that precisely that connection with the Tabernacle engendered the wedding image in all the above examples of this subgenre of the hasidic parable.

That connection is brought out clearly and emphatically in the homiletic exegesis on the Tabernacle found in the Zohar, a text certainly known to the respective hasidic masters. According to the Zohar, with the construction of the Tabernacle, the various realms of the kabbalistic cosmos became united, and the Tabernacle itself then became the scene of the union of *yesod* and *malkhut,* representing the distinctly masculine and feminine aspects of the world of the *sefirot.*[6] In addition, since the Tabernacle was constructed in the likeness of both this world and the upper world, those two realms become fused in the Tabernacle.[7] The unity of all the parts that go together to comprise the Tabernacle is further interpreted as a unification of the many components—internal and external—that together form a single physical body and a single person. The various mitzvot likewise unite to comprise one whole, and the unity represented in the Tabernacle parallels the inner integration of a person who, through the observance of holy deeds, himself becomes unified.[8] It becomes more and more obvious that the Zohar grasped the construction of the Tabernacle as a human act undertaken for the purpose of reforging the unity of the cosmos. With the completion of the Tabernacle and the Shekhinah's dwelling within it, union then occurred also between the lower and higher realms.[9] Furthermore, through the Tabernacle, Moses effected a union of the Shekhinah—the most immanent dimension of the Divine—with the world below, as the Shekhinah became, as it were, the bride of Moses.[10] And the Zohar explains the purpose of having a beautifully decorated canopy for a bride as giving honor to the Shekhinah, the Bride of the higher realm, who is present and participates in the joy of a human bride at her wedding and who, with the completion of the Tabernacle, unites with the world.[11] The meaning and effect of the Tabernacle are described in terms that mirror human love, marriage, and union,[12] and the Zohar views the Temple in Jerusalem as a site of unification between the two *sefirot*—*tiferet* and *malkhut*—just as it interpreted important Jewish liturgical moments in the same way.[13]

These zoharic teachings, in turn, echo as well as transform certain traditions preserved in the midrashic literature. These midrashic passages interpret the construction of the Tabernacle as a wedding either between God and the people of Israel or between Israel and the Torah (sometimes identified as the daughter of God). In the verse, "On the day that Moses finished (*kalot*) setting up the Tabernacle . . ." (Num. 7:1), the letters of the word *kalot* can also be read as *kalat* (bride). On the basis of that playful alternative vocalization of the unpointed text, a midrash in *Be-midbar rabbah* interprets the construction and setting up of the Tabernacle as a wedding between Israel and the Torah,[14] and the medieval commentator Rashi wrote on that same verse, "On the day that the Tabernacle was erected, Israel was like a bride who enters the marriage canopy."[15] Another tradition is more emphatic, as it adds, ". . . *kalat*, bride, referring to that day when Israel entered the bridal chamber as God's bride."[16]

The midrashic theme of the completion and dedication of the Tabernacle as a wedding between God and Israel appears to echo even earlier associations rooted in ancient conceptions of a temple as the scene of a sacred marriage. That conception from prebiblical religion—one echoed much more explicitly in the Zohar's interpretations of both Tabernacle and Temple—is evident in much that has become uncovered of the religious life of the ancient Near East. Evidence from ancient love songs and art, especially from Mesopotamia, points to such ancient rites and myths[17]—rituals in which the king and queen themselves may have participated.[18] In ancient Sumer, it would appear that a priestess acted out the role of a goddess in the sacred marriage rite,[19] while in Babylon the new year festival was associated with a sacred marriage of the Babylonian gods Marduk and Ishtar.[20] The ancient temple was regarded as a nuptial chamber and scene of the divine wedding feast, for the purpose of encouraging and ensuring the earth's fruitfulness.[21] Marriage ceremonies were enacted, as such rites would precede fertility.[22] Also among the Canaanites, evidence suggests sacred marriage rites in which the king or queen, or sometimes a priest and priestess, represented the gods.[23] Similar rituals were also practiced in Egypt and Greece.[24] Such rites expressed an urgent concern for survival in what was often a harsh environment. It was believed that the need for human, vegetative, and animal fertility and fruitfulness depended upon such rites of sacred marriage and the consequent sexual union between a god and goddess.[25]

The midrashic tradition likening the construction of the Tabernacle to a wedding appears as a refinement of just such older roots and a displacement of the earlier, pagan conception of the Temple as a divine, mythic nuptial chamber along with cultic sexual rites that would be utterly abhorrent in the eyes of biblical religion.[26]

This distant layer of associations, rooted in pagan religious consciousness and its conception of the Temple as the scene of sacred marriage, echoes even as it was translated and radically transformed into a very different mode of religious thought[27] voiced in the midrashic sources and later expressed more transparently in the Zohar.[28] And the same roots, going back to antiquity, are further transformed in the various hasidic parables translated above.

None of these hasidic parables conveys or even alludes to that mythic conception of the Temple (or Tabernacle) as a scene of marriage. In fact, it is significant that in those parables it is not the Temple and its specially hallowed space nor the building of the Tabernacle, but rather the entirety of a person's life in this world that is likened to a wedding. In accordance with an important aspect of the ethos of Hasidism, the parables' use of that talmudic saying, "The world can be likened to a wedding celebration," served to define the scene of the wedding neither in relation to a place nor an event of cultic worship, but rather in relation to all of life and to all the world.[29] Ancient, even prebiblical roots and associations echo in the hasidic parables quoted above, as they have been transformed to voice something of the particular spiritual world of classical Hasidism.

1. *Likkute Moharan tinyana*, #34.

2. A paraphrase of B. Eruvin 54a, *olma de'azlinan mine ke-hilula dame* (the world from which we will depart is similar to a wedding feast).

3. *Kedushat Levi ha-shalem*, (1993), "Likkutim, Aggadot Hazal," pp. 501–502.

4. *Degel mahane Efrayim* (1963), p. 119, Terumah.

5. *Toledot Ya'akov Yosef* (1973), Va-yakhel, 1:249.

6. Zohar 2:127a; *Zohar hadash*, *Midrash Ekha*, quoted in Raphael Patai, *Man and Temple in Ancient Jewish Myth and Ritual*, pp. 92–93.

7. Zohar 2:127a.

8. Ibid., 2:162b.

9. Ibid., 2:134b.

10. Ibid., 2:145a.

11. Ibid., 2:169a.
12. See Aryeh Wineman, *Mystic Tales from the Zohar*, 1997, pp. 96–99, in reference to the zoharic story "The Bridegroom's Silence." The theme of sacred marriage in relation to the theosophical, kabbalistic conception of the Divine, without particular reference to the Tabernacle or Temple, is discussed in Gershom Scholem's "The Feminine Element in Divinity," included in the collection of Scholem's essays, *On the Mystical Shape of the Godhead*, pp. 140–196.
13. Isaiah Tishby, *Mishnat ha-zohar*, vol. 2, pt. 2, *Avodat ha-kodesh*, pp. 183–578.
14. *Be-midbar rabbah* 12:8.
15. Note also *Shir ha-shirim rabbah* on Song of Songs 3:11.
16. *Pesikta derav Kahana*, ed. Solomon Buber, *Piska* 1, #5.
17. Marvin Pope, *Song of Songs: A New Translation*, p. 210.
18. Ibid., p. 373.
19. Ibid., p. 69.
20. Ibid., p. 81, n. 6.
21. Raphael Patai, *Man and Temple*, p. 88.
22. Ibid., p. 13.
23. Ibid., p. 89.
24. Ibid., p. 89.
25. Ibid., p. 13, drawing upon George Frazer, *The Golden Bough*, and p. 66.
26. That conception of the temple as a nuptial chamber may be alluded to in a comment found in *Shir ha-shirim rabbah* 1:16.2–3 in which *arsenu re'anana* (our leafy or verdant couch; Song of Songs 1:16) is identified as the Temple (also Song 3:7 as interpreted in *Tanhuma be-midbar*, ed. Solomon Buber, p. 33); and in the *Targum*, which interprets the verse that follows (Song 1:17) in terms of the structure of the messianic Temple. See Marvin Pope, *Song of Songs*, pp. 360, 362; and Raphael Patai, *Man and T   e   m   p   l   e   ,* pp. 90–91.
27. Samuel Henry Hooke (*Myth and Ritual*, p. 85) suggested that this theme was spiritualized in biblical religion in the image of Israel's Divine Husband.
28. The zoharic author understood the biblical Song of Songs as "a nuptial hymn of the Godhead itself" (Gershom Scholem, *On the Mystical Shape of the Godhead*, p. 194).
29. It is significant that while hasidic teaching continued to refer to the earlier kabbalistic theme of the union of *tiferet* and *malkhut* (Shekhinah), the sense of that unification is transformed to a life in which the human soul, through *devekut*, is united with its Divine Source. Note the passage in *Or ha-emet* (1899), 36b, in which the Maggid, Dov Baer of Mezherich—in speaking of the soul as "a portion of God above" and of the goal of a complete attachment of the portion to the Source—goes on to explain, "And *this* is the union of the Holy One, blessed be He *(tiferet)*, and the Shekhinah *(malkhut)*."

The Exiled Prince and the
Gem on the Ocean Floor:
A Parable Tradition

∽

I heard a parable concerning a prince whose father sent him away to a village in order that afterward the son might appreciate and take delight in the table of his father, the king. But due to his folly, the son joined with the villagers and learned from their deeds and forgot the royal delights. So the king sent his ministers to bring him back, but none succeeded in this until one of the ministers decided to act wisely and exchange his court garments for common clothing similar to what the villagers wear, and he succeeded [in bringing back the son to his father, the king]. *(Toledot Ya'akov Yosef)* [1]

Unlike most of the parables found in classical hasidic sources—parables that were contrived for their particular context in the discourses and sermons of the hasidic masters—the above parable has the marks of an older story, a type of quest tale, a staple of folk literature, adopted by the early hasidic preachers or teachers for their own purposes. While disguise—a familiar folktale motif—is generally for the sake of cunning or personal advantage, in this parable by Rabbi Ya'akov Yosef of Polonnoye, disguise is a strategy utilized in a task that is deemed holy.

This parable assumes the polarity of the royal court and the village, each with its own kinds of delights. The father's purpose is frustrated by the son's gravitation toward the life of the village. True to the traits of the

118

folktale genre and its strategy of building and maintaining tension, the wise minister who comes upon a new strategy is the last one of the series of ministers.[2]

Following a somewhat abbreviated form of the same parable story that appears elsewhere in the same text, Rabbi Ya'akov Yosef of Polonnoye explains that the village in the parable refers to "this lowly world." As his source for that interpretation, the author quotes the Zohar's parable of death (mentioned in the Introduction, p. xiv):

> A king has a son whom he sent away to a village to grow up there until he might be able to learn the ways of the royal palace. When the king hears that his son has grown up, what does he do? Out of love for his son, he sends the boy's mother—the matron, a woman of rank— to bring him up to the palace, so that there he might rejoice daily in his son's company.[3]

The zoharic source goes on to identify the son as the higher holy soul which the King (the Holy One, blessed be He) sent to this world so that there he might grow up and learn the ways of the Royal Palace.

The reader might be tempted to assume a direct connection between the hasidic parables of the king's son sent away from the royal palace and the earlier parable of death found in the Zohar. But though sharing several key elements with that zoharic parable, the hasidic parable quoted above contains two significant motifs not present in the zoharic parable: forgetting and the change of garments. And going back many centuries, both of these motifs, curiously, are present in an ancient source that appears to serve as the closest analogue of the parable cited above from the writings of Rabbi Ya'akov Yosef of Polonnoye. That source, generally known today as the "Hymn of the Pearl," is found in the *Acts of the Apostle Thomas,* an apocryphal Christian work probably written in Syriac in the second century C.E.

In that ancient gnostic text, a king sends his child on a journey during the course of which the son's royal robe together with his purple mantle are taken from him. The child's mission directs him to descend to Egypt (this lower world) for the purpose of bringing up from the sea a pearl guarded by a serpent. During his dangerous journey to Egypt, the prince stays at an inn where others (strangers) are also staying. He tries to remember his mission and maintain his sense of identity but, fearful of his new neighbors, he begins to wear their kind of garments, befriends them, and eats meat and drinks with them. He then forgets his identity as a prince and he forgets the pearl that he had been sent to obtain. As a result of his abundant eating and drinking, a deep sleep falls upon him.

Grieved at their son's forgetting, his parents write a letter to awaken him—a letter in which they recall to him his identity as a prince, enlighten him as to his present state of enslavement, and remind him both of his mission to fetch the pearl and of the robe and mantle that have been taken from him. The letter is itself a messenger that assumes the form of an eagle that flies and speaks. The son then proceeds to charm the serpent and seizes the pearl with which he returns home. There he removes his impure garment and puts on his original mantle and robe, which he understands to be his own mirror image. The account concludes as his father receives his son with great joy.[4]

The ancient gnostic myth shares with the eighteenth-century hasidic parable the motifs of forgetting and of the change of garments. An additional element—the letter, included in the "Hymn of the Pearl"—figures boldly in a variation of the same hasidic parable, also found in one of the homilies of Rabbi Ya'akov Yosef of Polonnoye.

A king's only son was held in a very difficult captivity. A long time passed but the king retained the hope of eventually redeeming his son and restoring him to himself, and after many years a letter from his father, the king, reached the son, telling him not to despair there and not to forget the manners of royalty while among the wild wolves of the plain, for the father's hand is still readied to restore the son to himself. . . . (*Toledot Ya'akov Yosef*)[5]

Another motif—the quest for the gem in the seas—found in the gnostic "Hymn of the Pearl" also distinctly recalls a rather similar story type found repeatedly in hasidic parables. We note also in *Toledot Ya'akov Yosef*, for example, "a parable of the king who lost a precious stone in the depths of the sea, and he had to send his sons there [to find it]. . . ."[6] Sometimes the motifs of the exiled prince and the gem in the sea appear together in the very same parable, and more often the two motifs relate to the very same themes. It would seem that while the hasidic parables were influenced by that parable in the Zohar, they also drew from a much older tradition with roots found already in the ancient world and reflected in ancient gnostic lore. The similarity of motifs and story type with the "Hymn of the Pearl" can make no claim concerning either the kinds of oral literary sources that reached eighteenth-century Hasidism or the channels of transmission, but they do indicate the antiquity of the motif cluster, comprising what came to be a hasidic parable tradition. The themes found in ancient Gnosticism could well reflect mythic patterns and motifs that were actually much more widely dispersed and not at all unique to Gnosticism.[7] The basic parable type that we have noted appears in numerous variations in classical hasidic texts, but more significant than the occurrence of variations is the range of applications associated with the same basic parable. This multiplicity of meanings further suggests that Hasidism utilized a much older source, providing it with its own multiple interpretations.

Let us note some of the ways in which these motifs of the exiled prince and the gem on the ocean floor were molded and interpreted in various hasidic sources. Rabbi Ya'akov Yosef of Polonnoye repeatedly refers to the motif of the king's minister who changed his garb in order to connect with the king's banished son and return him to his father. He explains the minister's change of garb as symbolizing a strategy designed to reach the multitudes and elevate them to a higher level of holiness. To influence those immersed in material concern and to raise them to an essentially higher level characterized by mind and spirit, it is necessary first to descend to their level in order to connect with them.[8] In the parable, only the change of garments enables the minister to connect with the prince and "to speak to his heart" so that he may then be able to influence the prince to return to his father.[9] In descending to a lower level for that pur-

pose, the minister exchanges his own court garments—symbols of his status—for the clothing of commoners. The *nimshal* makes it clear that the
person standing on that lower level, more earthly and distanced from the
spiritual, is nonetheless worthy of the love and effort necessary to bring
him nearer to the Torah.[10]

Elsewhere in the same collection of homilies,[11] Rabbi Ya'akov Yosef
interprets the directions to the priests found in Ezekiel 44 as a similar
model of spiritual leadership. In that biblical text the priests are ordered
to remove their priestly robes, an act which suggests to Rabbi Ya'akov
Yosef the strategy of the wise minister who removes his royal garb to connect with the prince. The priests, Ya'akov Yosef explains, were unable to
hallow the people while clad in their priestly robes. Furthermore, the
priests were then to proceed to the outer court, leaving the inner court, a
detail which suggests to Ya'akov Yosef the need to leave the isolation of
an uninterrupted higher spiritual and intellectual level in order to make
contact with those on a lower, more material level.

Rabbi Ya'akov Yosef interprets the clothes as qualities, evoking the
thought that it is necessary for a spiritual teacher to descend in order to
assume, at least symbolically, the qualities of the larger populace in the
hope of elevating the multitudes to a higher level.[12] And while the village
represents the spiritually and intellectually lower strata among Jews, nevertheless, in the same passage[13] the villagers are described as "children of
kings," an apparent paradox suggesting that the evident condition of the
villagers does not reflect their true identity. As royalty in exile, efforts
must be made to reach them and bring them up to their true, higher level.
In some examples of the parable, the son is captured,[14] while more often
the king himself sends his son (described often as his only son or his
beloved son) to the village "that he might acquire greater desire for the
table of his father, the king."[15] The king's strategy, however, fails in that
the son, rather than acquiring a greater appreciation of the palace life,
erases it from his mind and completely acculturates to the life of the village and its lower level of values.

Sent to influence the alienated son, the king's minister confronts the
very same danger to which the prince had succumbed. What if, in
descending to a lower level, he becomes trapped there without returning
to his own prior, higher level?[16] Rabbi Ya'akov Yosef counsels such a per-

son that before going down to the pit one should bring with him a ladder with which, if necessary, to climb out of the pit.[17] One must have a firm sense of one's own values before making that descent to connect with the exiled prince or with the larger Jewish populace.

Through these parables, Rabbi Ya'akov Yosef of Polonnoye was expressing his criticism of the established Jewish religious leadership and was emphasizing the need for an alternative mode of spiritual leadership. He envisioned a leadership that would not be indifferent and distant from the Jewish multitudes but rather concerned to make the effort to connect with them. Only through such connection could a leader succeed in elevating them to a higher level. Doing so, however, necessitates a surrender of the isolation and detachment enjoyed by the more conventional and official Jewish religious leadership (the rabbinate and the talmudic scholars of the yeshivah).[18]

A reshuffling of the same cluster of motifs is evident in the following brief parable related by the Maggid, Dov Baer of Mezherich.

> A king's son goes among the villagers to seek a treasure that is with [or belongs to] a villager. And behold he has to dress like a villager so that they will not recognize that he is a king's son, so that they might disclose to him their secrets including the location of the treasure. (*Maggid devarav le-Ya'akov*)[19]

In this version—explaining why a holy man will sometimes descend to the level of seemingly petty conversation—the prince himself is engaged in the quest, and to succeed he must resort to the same strategy of maintaining a disguise. The treasure is found with a villager who is, in one sense, but a mask for a truer and higher identity.

Along with these parables' specific sociological and cultural meanings in the context of Hasidism's early history, that same motif pattern of descent and the danger associated with it bear overtones of the pattern of the quest myth exemplified in several medieval European romances. The quest brings the hero figure into the underworld and sets up his confrontation with death, the descent being a requirement for the hero's own awakening and renewal.[20] The overtones of the romance and of the traditional quest tales implicit in the hasidic parable of this type might subtly suggest that the descent to the lower level of the Jewish masses is an absolute prerequisite for spiritual rebirth on the part of the Torah student himself.

The accent in this parable, however, is placed upon the treasure— upon the person whose real worth is concealed and is revealed only when, with the help of the hero in quest, he is elevated to the level of a truer relationship with God.

Proposing and also exemplifying a new mode of spiritual leadership was of utmost concern to the early hasidic teachers. The complex of elements in the parable tradition under discussion, nevertheless, was made to relate also to several other themes in classical hasidic teaching. Variations including structural changes of the parable types point to different meanings. The following version of this same motif, for example, beyond the similarity of its opening lines, is marked by some significant differences.

> A parable of a king whose only son was captured in an exceedingly difficult captivity. . . . Much time passed but [the father] retained his hope that his son might be liberated and restored to him. And following many years, a letter from his father, the king, reaches the son, encouraging him not to despair there and not to forget the courteous ways of the royal palace even while he is among the wolves of the plain, for the father is preparing to return the son to him through many tactics both of war and peace, and the like. The king's son at once experiences great joy, but since the letter has to be kept a secret, it is impossible for him to openly rejoice in his father's letter. What does he do? He goes with his townspeople to a wine tavern where the others experi-

ence a physical joy in the wine while he rejoices in his
father's letter. . . ." (Toledot Ya'akov Yosef)[21]

A series of polarities is evident in the above parable story: hope and
despair, remembering and forgetting, along with openness and concealment. The *nimshal* draws a parallel with the physical delights of the
Shabbat, including eating and drinking, which make it possible for the
devout person to experience a different type of joy, spiritual in nature. In
still another homily in the same work[22] the material delights of the
Shabbat are said to comprise an external type of joy, while the spiritual
delight is a joy of an inner nature extending to the very essence of the
Shabbat. Both types of joy are important. One must not focus upon spiritual delight to the exclusion of the more external physical delights and
needs, for the fulfillment that is spiritual in nature is not possible without
the physical delights of the holy day. At the same time, it is clear that the
one comes strictly for the sake of making the other possible.

In another homily found in the same collection,[23] Rabbi Ya'akov Yosef
makes it clear that the parable of the letter sent to the captive son relates
to the dichotomy between matter and form as they exist within the very
same person. The Maggid of Mezherich relates the following version of
this parable type.

A king's son is taken captive alongside one of the servants, a frivolous person who takes to hilarity and drink.
The son wishes to think of his father that his father
might also remember him. What does that son do? He
connects his thoughts with the delight of knowing that
his father engages always in his royal practices. Now the
frivolous servant wants to drink wine and become
drunk, and the prince fears that the captive might flee;
so he goes to drink with him. But while the two of them
are both drinking and going about gleefully, their moti-

vations are not the same. Though the king's son goes
joyfully to the tavern, his intent is not for the sensual
delight of the feast; for if it were he would not be connecting his thought with that of his father—as a king is
not accustomed to take to drinking wine—rather his real
thought is that in this way he might experience delight
and joy and be able to connect, in his thoughts, with his
father, and he is thinking of his father. But the servant's
joy in going to the tavern is, rather, for the physical
pleasure of drinking itself. *(Maggid devarav le-Ya'akov)*[24]

The situation of the prince in this parable recalls the hasidic concept of
avodah be-gashmi'ut, retaining an inner mental attachment to God even
while fulfilling the physical activities that life requires.

The letter motif together with the theme of remembering and forgetting are both present in a parable told by Rabbi Hayyim
Halberstamm of Zanz concerning a prince who was punished by being
sent away from home.

A king's son sins against his father who then sends
him away from home. So long as the prince is still in
proximity to his home, people recognize him and treat
him kindly, providing him with food and drink because
he is the king's son. But afterwards as he wanders further into his father's realm, people no longer recognize
him at all, and he has nothing. He begins to sell his rai-
ment in order to purchase food. In time, he no longer
has garments to sell, and so in order to eat he begins
working as a shepherd. So once again he lacks nothing.
He wears only the simplest and most basic attire; he
stays with the sheep, tending them on the mountains,

and he sings there as do the other shepherds, and he completely forgets that he was once a prince along with the delights to which he was formerly accustomed.

It is the custom of shepherds to make for themselves a small straw roof to protect them from the rain, so he seeks to make for himself such a small roof, but he lacks the means to do so. And he becomes very sad. One day the king is passing through that land, and it is the custom that when a king passes through the land, whoever has a request writes his request for the king on a piece of paper and throws it inside the king's chariot. The king's son comes among the others and throws his request, written on paper, that he wants a small straw roof as the shepherds make. The king recognizes his son's handwriting and he is distressed that his son has fallen to such a level that he has forgotten that he is a king's son and he feels the need only for a straw roof.

By way of the *nimshal*, Rabbi Hayyim of Zanz added:

This is the situation today in the world. We have already forgotten that each one is a prince; we have forgotten what we truly lack. One person cries that he needs a livelihood, and another cries for children, while concerning our true need for the precious delights that we knew in days of old—for these we totally forget to pray. (*Sefer darke ḥayyim*)[25]

In this parable, constructed between the poles of recognition and forgetting, the exiled prince finds himself further and further distant from the palace, both geographically and psychologically. Exile is associated with distancing and forgetting and is ultimately equivalent to a loss of identity. When no one recognizes him, he in turn ceases to know himself and undergoes a loss of identity. For money to purchase food he sells his royal clothing, the court clothing that served to distinguish him from the other shepherds. In this story, the shepherds play the role of the villagers or the comrades at the inn found in other parables.

The prince, who lives and works and defines his needs exactly as do other shepherds, fully assumes a shepherd's identity. Also in the practice of writing requests to the king, he does as they do, conforming to their practice. It is the king who remembers, recognizing his son's handwriting, while his son recognizes neither his own identity nor his father. In a reversal of roles evident from the prevalent pattern of the letter motif, the letter—or in this case a written request—is sent by the son to the father. The story is intentionally fragmented and concludes before the son's presumed return to suggest that each person writes such a letter in his own consciousness as he delineates his needs and through them his sense of identity.

These parables pose the question, "How should one define one's own true identity?" Does one identify essentially with one's body, one's transitory garment and its needs, or with a deeper aspect of one's being? Do the connotations of the village or the royal palace symbolize one's ultimate identity? This parable aims at a transformation of consciousness; one equated, however, with a realization of what a person has, in truth, always been.[26]

Motifs from this parable tradition acquire still another form in this parable told by the Maggid of Mezherich.

A person should not feel exalted because he prays with inner devotion [kavvanah]. For he is merely like a villager who normally is never permitted even to come into the king's presence. But when a son of the king is lost, and that villager brings a letter from the son, then the guards not only allow him to enter without difficulty but they themselves bring him before the king. *(Maggid devarav le-Ya'akov)*[27]

In this brief parable, it is a villager who brings to the king a letter from the latter's lost son and who is hence most welcome at the royal court. The *nimshal* informs the reader that the king's lost son represents an extraneous, disturbing thought that contains, however, a captive Holy Spark. In this hasidic concept—as has already been noted—every thought in its deeper nature is considered to be an aspect of Divinity, and even the most perverse and unwelcome thought is a distorted form of what is actually holy. The parable tradition concerning the banished or captive or lost prince is here understood as the redemption of such a "strange thought" containing a Holy Spark, which calls out to the person to redeem it so that the spark may be reunited with its Divine Source. The figure of the villager who restores the lost prince to his father mirrors a universal human situation: Each person in life, in receiving such an extraneous thought, has, in the process, descended to the level of the villager; but nonetheless he is able, on that level, to fulfill his task of redeeming the fallen spark and, in doing so, bring joy to the King.

Elsewhere, the Maggid relates the parable of the lost gem at the bottom of the sea in this rather surprising way.

A parable of a king who lost a precious stone from his ring at a time when he had countless servants and ministers and soldiers of various ranks in his court. But despite that fact, he does not wish to order them to seek that gem; rather he commands only his beloved son to seek and find the lost object and restore it to his father, the king. And though the king could trust each and every one of his ministers and servants—that, upon finding it, they would return it to him in good condition—nevertheless it is not his will that they should search for it, for he wishes to bestow the merit [of finding it] on his cherished son, wishing him to receive credit for the find. Furthermore he even alludes to his beloved son in various ways concerning its location. For the loss had occurred intentionally, and the king knows its location, and he arranged everything only in order to be able to give credit to his beloved son and to know the delight from his son's finding it, boasting that no one in the world could have searched and found it other than his son whom he loves. *(Likkutim yekarim)*[28]

The nature of the task, which recalls the "Hymn of the Pearl," is present in a series of folktale motifs,[29] which, though not found in classical rabbinic texts, do appear in the hasidic parables. The gem, connoting brightness, contrasts with the sea, which suggests both darkness and chaos and the primordial formless matter. The finding of the gem might suggest the transformation of darkness into light—the metamorphosis of a human life from a chaotic state to one marked by form and direction.[30] Though the familiar motif of a serpent guarding the treasure[31] is not present in these parables, the water has overtones not dissimilar from those of a demonic creature guarding the treasure; the water not only conceals the gem but also serves as a place of danger that the hero, accepting his task, must confront.[32]

The *nimshal* identifies the gem with the fallen Divine Sparks; and the role of the *tzaddik* (the holy man) is defined in terms of his task of gathering and raising up those Holy Sparks. The sting of the earlier Lurianic concept is clearly muted in that the sparks are not really lost; the loss is only apparent and even contrived, and the king is able to intimate to his son the location of the gem. The gathering of those sparks, nevertheless, is the reason for the soul's descent to this material existence and hence defines the meaning of human existence. It is precisely in the depths of the sea—in the material universe suggesting a remoteness from the Divine—that the gem and the fallen sparks are located. The *tzaddik* is one who grasps and fulfills the human, holy task within this material realm of being. And as is made clear in the *nimshal*, the task of seeking the fallen Holy Sparks is given not to the angels, but to man.

The ancient motif of the gem located in the depth of the sea—whatever the actual sources and transmission of the motif—also radiates in hasidic parables in a way to allude to contrasting approaches to Jewish religious life within Eastern European Jewry—specifically to early Hasidism's understanding of itself in contrast with the more conventional modes of Jewish religious life and study.

> A parable of a king who lost a precious stone of immense worth and feared to send his servants to find it, preferring to send his son[s] instead. And among them were three very different types: one made a real effort, devoting all his energy to locate the precious stone; the second cried out to his father, etc.; while the third remained there in the depths of the sea. (*Toledot Ya'akov Yosef*)[33]

In the context of the above parable, Rabbi Ya'akov Yosef of Polonnoye speaks of different levels of the Torah and of individuals who relate to those various levels. Some make a garment for themselves to wear in the lower Paradise, a garment woven of the plain meanings of the Torah and the mitzvot. Others, penetrating more to the intent of the Torah and its holy deeds, make for themselves a more superior garment to wear in the upper Paradise. And others prepare a crown out of acts of unification— acts done with devotion and intent to effect union within the self and within the higher realms of being. Still others, in contrast, either fail to prepare any kind of garment or, through their transgressions, weave for themselves a sordid garment. The entire Torah with its mitzvot, Rabbi Ya'akov Yosef explains, was given for the purpose of our redeeming the fallen Holy Sparks that, with *shevirat ha-kelim* (the Shattering of the Vessels), fell into the depths, just as the precious stone in the parable was cast down to the depths of the sea. The parable in that homily continues:

> But when the king observed that [those sent for the task] were in no hurry to proceed to find the gem, he decided to scatter also coins of silver and gold and pen-

nies [34] as well so that they would seek those coins, in the process of which they might come upon the precious stone. . . .

The quest for the fallen Divine Sparks, Rabbi Ya'akov Yosef explains, concerns the esoteric level of the Torah, which alone signifies the Torah's real purpose. Though not negated in any sense, the more exoteric matrix of Torah and mitzvot, it is implied, is to be regarded not as an end in itself but rather as a guide in finding the gem, the *sod* (mystery), which comprises the deepest level of meaning in the Torah.

Another retelling of the same parable included within the same collection of homilies[35] delineates its criticism somewhat differently. There, of the three kinds of sons, one feels that his father has simply sent him away, and so, angrily, he remains in the sea depths without making any effort to seek the gem. The second son simply wishes to return to his father and does nothing, while the third son understands that he was sent to the depths for a purpose, so he searches and finds the gem and joyfully brings it back to his father.

Pondering the varied responses of the king's three sons, the reader perceives in the first son an anger that gives rise to cynicism. He succumbs to the evil husk of the extraneous thought. The second son avoids that level of descent and will do nothing to close the door to the possibility of his returning home, but beyond that he will do nothing positive in nature. This type of son might well represent the mindless and perfunctory observance that classical Hasidism repeatedly criticized—a type of observance intent on fulfilling the demands of the law without any inner enthusiasm or soul involvement. The third son, in contrast with his two brothers, seriously goes about his task and succeeds in locating the gem. Only the third son raises the exiled fallen sparks, and the reader understands that the homilist identifies the third son as a follower of the hasidic path.

A variant of that pattern is found in a parable told by the Maggid of Mezherich:

A parable of a king who lost his seal, and the loss of a royal seal is great indeed, for whoever finds it will be able to use the seal to sign [pronouncements] in the name of the king. And it is also an embarrassment that the king's seal lies in the dust. The king is distressed that his seal is lost, and the ministers are saddened because the seal of their king is lost. And they all go to search, and precisely because of their eagerness, they pass right by it and fail to find it. A villager goes and finds it. Now the villager, who does not understand the importance of the seal, nevertheless brings joy to all of them. The king rejoices that his seal was found, and similarly all of them rejoice, and the villager rejoices in having found the royal seal even though he does not grasp its significance; but nevertheless he rejoices in that the seal belongs to the king. . . . (*Likkutim yekarim*) [36]

Familiar with the connotations of the village as representing the earthiness of this world and a remoteness from spiritual life and concern, the reader cannot fail to note that in this parable the villager is regarded in a most positive light. Though he is unlearned, he has proved himself a model of true devotion. In this parable it is difficult not to overhear a social and ideological claim that for all their knowledge and erudition, members of the rabbinic elite may have missed the essential core of the whole enterprise of Torah study and that in the final analysis devotion without learning is preferable to learning without devotion. It is ultimately through the dimension of devotion—accessible to all—that the king's gem is found.

Voicing this same parable tradition, Menahem Nahum of Chernobyl, in *Me'or einayim* on Exodus, remarked that "when a man is standing upon a roof and a precious stone lies on the ground, he is unable to take it unless he goes down to its place." [37] Menahem Nahum relates that parable image to his concept of the necessity of the Israelites to descend to Egypt in order to raise up the Holy Letters of Torah (in its pre-Sinaitic state), which had fallen into exile among the lower shells of being, equated with *Mitzrayim* (Egypt).

On a more individual level, Menahem Nahum, in the same passage, recalls to his hearers and readers the Lurianic concept that prior to the sin of Adam, the first man contained the totality of human souls, which then fell to the depths with the shells. Each person, consequently, has the task of raising up his own soul from the *kelipot* (shells) by grasping, beyond the material garments of being, the Divine Presence within and beyond all that is, and by effecting, in this sense, a oneness of the earthly and the heavenly. The gem on the sea floor is understood as the holiness subtly present in and underlying what is seemingly worldly. Underlying Menahem Nahum's worldview is that recurring image that translates into the suggestion that each and every person is, in reality, the king's son sent on a mission to locate the gem and restore it to the king.

The motif of the quest for the gem on the floor of the sea is referred to in a homily[38] in which the Maggid of Mezherich interprets the biblical story of Joseph as a universal, recurrent happening suspended between the opposite poles of remembering and forgetting. The purpose of man's coming to this world, the Maggid states, is to serve God in a world of earthliness and physicality suggested by the sea depths. The *tzaddik* (righteous and holy person) remembers to fulfill this task in life while the *rasha* (wicked) forgets, thinking instead only of material desires. The familiar parable is overheard as the implicit, deeper meaning of the biblical Joseph story.

The motif of forgetting and remembering resonates a significant paradoxical strand of thought in the teaching of the Maggid, Dov Baer of Mezherich. According to the Maggid, forgetting the true Root of all existence—forgetting that neither the self nor the world has any existence apart from the Divine—is a necessity insofar as without such forgetting the world could have no existence. Such forgetting, represented by the king's son forgetting his own identity and equated with the Shattering of the Vessels, is the flawed consciousness in which concrete, physical reality is rooted. Without that forgetting, no existence on any level would be possible other than that of *Ein Sof*—the completely infinite, unbounded and incomprehensible state of the Divine. The very existence of the cosmos is hence founded upon a measure of illusion in the form of forgetting. However, the way of *avodah*—of true worship and relatedness to the Divine in life—is a potentially acosmic counterprocess that, to a degree, annuls that fundamental and necessary forgetting. While forgetting has an indispensable place in the economy of existence, spiritual realization seriously qualifies the impact of forgetting.[39]

The motif of the minister who, by changing his clothing and way of speaking, is able to make connection with the king's son on his present level and hence succeeds in bringing him back to his father, appears in a late eighteenth-century text in the name of the Baal Shem Tov. As in the previous statements of this motif that we have already met, this wise minister, through his ingenuity, succeeds after others sent by the king had failed. In that text—*Keter shem tov*—a single line comprises the *nimshal* following the parable story: "And this is the cladding of the Torah in material stories."[40] While the text, edited by Aharon Zevi ben Meir ha-kohen of Apt, attributes the parable to the Besht, the brief *nimshal* would suggest a strong affinity with a viewpoint prevalent in the teachings of the Maggid of Mezherich: the narratives found in the Torah—stories set within this physical world and level of existence; stories that occur within time—are not consonant with a higher, and hence truer, level of the Torah. The Torah as Divine Wisdom itself—the Torah that preceded the coming into being of a material plane of being and exists on a higher, nonmaterial plane—would not include narratives that occur within time. But the human being as a creature of this world would be unable to relate to the Torah as it exists in such a higher, spiritual state, just as the king's son, attuned to the life of the village, does not relate to the attempts of the king's other ministers to bring him back to his father until the arrival of the one wise minister dressed as a villager. This level of existence, represented by the village, requires that the Torah, in its higher form, be translated into a material form. Its truth, transcending time, must be translated into a world structured in terms of time. The true essence of the Torah requires garments appropriate to the nature of this lower experiential world, and so the Torah, as known on a human plane, is clad "in material stories."[41]

As an older, inherited narrative tradition with roots predating Hasidism, the motifs of the exiled prince and the gem on the floor of the sea could be held up and turned around at different angles to the light of hasidic thought and, in the process, could be freely restructured to voice a considerable range of diverse meanings, all of them significant themes in classical hasidic teaching. Unlike examples of the more original hasidic parables, invented to express a particular concept, a parable tradition reflecting such older roots more naturally lends itself to a significant openness of meaning. The attempt to trace the multiple functions and interpretation of these parables in the hasidic homily is a journey through key aspects of the hasidic ethos.

---

1. *Toledot Ya'akov Yosef* (1973), Emor, 1:397.
2. Axel Olrik, "Epic Laws of Folk Narrative," p. 135.
3. Zohar 1:245b.
4. A translation of the Syriac text is included in Hans Jonas, *The Gnostic Religion,* pp. 113–116.
5. *Toledot Ya'akov Yosef* (1973), Kedoshim, 1:331.
6. Ibid., I, p. 429, Be-ḥukkotai.
7. Mircea Eliade, *A History of Religious Ideas,* vol. 2, p. 371.
8. *Toledot Ya'akov Yosef,* Yitro, 1:196.
9. Ibid., Bo, 1:145.
10. Ibid., Yitro, 1:197.
11. Ibid., Yitro, 1:199.
12. Ibid., Emor, 1:381.
13. Ibid., Emor, 1:397.
14. Ibid., Kedoshim, 1:331.
15. Ibid., Emor, 1:380–381.
16. Ibid., Emor, 1:381.
17. Ibid., Shofetim, 2:678.
18. This theme is emphasized in *The Zaddik,* Samuel H. Dresner's study of the writings of Ya'akov Yosef of Polonnoye.
19. *Maggid devarav le-Ya'akov* (1976), #40, p. 60.
20. David Adams Leeming, "Quests," in *The Encyclopedia of Religion,* 12:146–152.
21. *Toledot Ya'akov Yosef* (1973), Kedoshim, 1:331.
22. Ibid., Shofetim, 2:671.
23. Ibid., Be-har, 1:411.
24. *Maggid devarav le-Ya'akov* (1976), #74, pp. 127–128.
25. *Sefer darke ḥayyim* (1923), chap. 13. This parable is included in Shmuel Yosef Agnon's anthology, *Yamim nora'im,* p. 28; English translation, *Days of Awe,* pp. 22–24.
26. This same underlying pattern is found in many traditions. See Heinrich Zimmer, *Philosophies of India,* p. 308 (*Sankhya-sutras* 4.1); also pp. 5–8, 508–509 (*Saddhar-mapundarika,* "The Lotus of the True Law," 4. *Sacred Books of the East,* vol. XXI, pp. 98ff). These tales illuminate the role of the spiritual teacher as one who directs a person to cast off his state of ignorance and return to his own true intrinsic nature.
27. *Maggid devarav le-Ya'akov* (1976), #105, p. 183.
28. *Likkutim yekarim* (1974), #268.

29. Including the following, listed in Stith Thompson, *Motif-Index of Folk-Literature:* H1132, H1132.1, H1132.1.1, and H1132.1.7. See Dov Neuman (Noy), *Motif-Index of Talmudic-Midrashic Literature.*

30. Yoav Elstein ("*Margalit be-fi nahash,*" p. 188) traces, in connection with the pearl image, the association of the capacity of turning night into day.

31. See, for example, Stith Thompson, *Motif-Index of Folk-Literature:* B11.6.2, N570, B576.2, N570, B576.2, G354.1.1.

32. Juan Eduardo Cirlot, *A Dictionary of Symbols,* p. 365.

33. *Toledot Ya'akov Yosef* (1973), Emor, 1:384.

34. The coins can suggest riches of any sort, easily accessible and easily lost and sought out of selfish motivation. See Cirlot, *A Dictionary of Symbols,* p. 328.

35. *Toledot Ya'akov Yosef* (1973), Be-hukkotai, 1:429.

36. *Likkutim yekarim* (1974), #45.

37. Menahem Nahum of Chernobyl, *Me'or einayim,* Part 2, on Exodus (1984), 28a.

38. *Likkutim yekarim* (1974), #267.

39. See *Maggid devarav le-Ya'akov* (1976), #73.

40. *Keter shem tov* (1858), Part 1, 16a.

41. Note the discussion of this aspect of the Maggid's thinking in our Introduction.

THE
POLEMICS
OF AN
HOUR
OF
HISTORY

∽

Arms without Fire

～

*T*he king commands a servant to learn the tactics of war: how to hold a gun and how to position himself vis-à-vis those fighting against him in war and take aim at them. Now during the time of instruction, no fire is placed in the gun, for then there is no need for fire. But later this same man takes the weapon with him as he goes to war. He stands in the correct position and uses the weapon just as he had previously done while learning, without placing any fire in the weapon, while those fighting him easily defeat him and make mockery of him.

The *nimshal:* The Blessed One, blessed be His Name—who is entirely beyond the reach of thought—gave us a Torah in the form of black fire written upon white fire[1] so that with it we would be able to combat the Evil Inclination *(yetzer ha-ra)*. . . . And through the mitzvot that we perform with great enthusiasm and desire we can cleave to the very core of the mitzvah—which is white fire—distancing ourselves from what is material and approaching a grasp of the Creator. But whoever does these without enthusiasm but simply in a perfunctory way[2] is like that servant who, in war, fails to place fire in his weapons. . . . *(Kedushat Levi)*[3]

141

The parable's juxtaposing of military activity with worship, which might initially make for a jarring effect, exemplifies an aspect of the art and literary power of many hasidic parables in which *mashal* and *nimshal* appear to come from totally unrelated spheres of life, even areas of endeavor with sharply differing value patterns. The parallel between the two is explained and justified in the *nimshal* in that mitzvot comprise a way to engage in warfare against one's own negative qualities—against a negative aspect of one's own complex psychological makeup.

Rabbi Levi Yitzhak of Berdichev restates in parable form a basic theme in classical hasidic teaching: if one performs the commanded deeds and holy acts of the Torah tradition in a mindless manner, without feeling and enthusiasm, merely going through the correct motions, then those same deeds—like the weapon lacking firepower—are totally without effect. The goal is not simply the performance of the act itself, and the act cannot be divorced from the spirit in which the act is performed.

What is given in fire—to quote a most forceful midrashic image—must be lived in fire, in the fire of one's own innerness. The Hebrew word for "enthusiasm," *hitlahavut*, contains within it the smaller word, *lahav* (flame). Torah, lacking such fire, is only potential Torah, and in the eyes of the Berdichever a holy deed divorced from a reservoir of fervor, from a depth of love and awe, is a failed deed.

Eighteenth-century Hasidism was, in one sense, a protest against what it perceived as a prevalent mode of Torah study and religious observance divorced from a deeper dimension of spiritual experience. As the hasidic master perceived the larger religious landscape around him, attention to form had completely taken over, leaving little space for the spirit, for the experience of Divine Light and inner enthusiasm that must infuse and permeate the form. While in no way negating the crucial ingredients of Torah study and mitzvot in religious life, Hasidism emerged within the world of Jewish tradition and traditional society at a time and place when the forces of modernity expressed in Haskalah had not yet challenged that traditional milieu and its foundations. Its teachers insisted that both the study and the performance of holy deeds should be infused with spirituality, that they connect with a depth of religious experience. Both Torah study and the pattern of holy deeds are to serve as a means to *devekut* (an inner attachment to the Divine); they require a dimension of inwardness of the holy act itself. Some of the hasidic masters spoke of the capacity of the *tzaddik* to fulfill a mitzvah, both on the level of concrete deed and on the higher level of the root of the mitzvah transcending the concrete deed. In this parable, the Berdichever goes beyond criticism of the general scene of Jewish religious living to completely negate the value of study and mitzvot that fail to connect with a very real and intense awareness of God.[4]

This parable of Rabbi Levi Yitzhak of Berdichev reflects the critical position of his teacher, the Maggid of Mezherich, that the primary element in fulfilling a mitzvah is the *hitlahavut* (enthusiasm and inner fire) present in the deed. The actual deed itself is necessary simply because by its very nature, the spiritual fire—the inner intent and enthusiasm—requires a vessel to clothe it.[5] This position, reiterated in a number of the early hasidic texts, clearly defines the dimension of inner intent and devotion (*kavvanah*) as indispensable to the worth of any holy deed.

The above parable appears within a homiletic comment on a statement in Mishnah Avot attributed to Rabbi Yohanan ben Zakkai: "If you have learned much Torah, do not take credit for it, as it was for this purpose that you were brought into being."[6] The reader might be puzzled to note a link between this parable and its context, relating to that rabbinic statement. Rabbi Levi Yitzhak, however, points to the word *le-atzmekha* (to yourself; don't attribute this to yourself as a personal accomplishment), and explains the connection, providing a rather startling twist of reasoning: if you study Torah in such a manner that you have space also "for yourself," then your endeavor is self-contradictory in nature. The connection is understood rather than explicitly spelled out: Torah study, like true fulfillment of a holy deed performed with enthusiasm, with inner fire, leaves no space for self, for ego.

Two criticisms of the more normative religious scene merge together in the Berdichever's homily: a critique of mindless and perfunctory holy deeds and the accusation that in the world of talmudic learning as he perceived it—though the Berdichever was himself a talmudic scholar of note—study was often placed in the service of ego. These criticisms come together to illuminate the character of true spiritual fervor in that such spirituality allows no space for egotism. That inner fire, which Rabbi Levi Yitzhak demanded, and concern with considerations of self are mutually exclusive.

1. *Kemitzvat anashim melumdah* (*Shir ha-shirim rabbah* 5.11.6).
2. Isaiah 29:13.
3. *Kedushat Levi ha-shalem* (1993), *Likkutim, Masekhet avot,* p. 305.
4. In this respect, Rabbi Shneur Zalman, founder of the Ḥabad school of hasidic thought—who sought in significant ways to make Hasidism more palatable to the rabbinic authorities and who affirmed the significance of every mitzvah that is done, even if not carried out in the ideal spirit—differed from more mainstream classical hasidic teaching. See *Tanya* I, chap. 4, and Rivka Schatz Uffenheimer, *Hasidism as Mysticism,* pp. 256, 280–289, where the author describes the position of Rabbi Shneur Zalman as "anti-hasidic."
5. *Maggid devarav le-Ya'akov* (1976), #97, pp. 169–170. Also *Shemu'ah tovah,* 36b, quoted in Rivka Schatz Uffenheimer, *Hasidism as Mysticism,* p. 113.
6. M. Avot 2:9.

On the Inability to Hear the Melody

~

Someone plays a musical instrument very beautifully with such an exceedingly sweet sound that those who hear it are unable to restrain themselves. In their great joy they break out dancing, jumping almost to the ceiling as they are moved by the delight of the pleasant, sweet sounds. And the nearer one stands or the nearer one approaches, the greater the delight that person experiences, and he dances with exuberance.

And in the midst of this scene comes a deaf person, unable to hear anything of the sweet sound of the instrument. He sees the people dancing with tremendous energy and, hearing no sound, he considers them to be madmen, and he thinks, "What good is their merriment?"[1] But if he is wise and realizes that people are dancing because of the very delightful and pleasant sound of the musical instrument, he himself would join with them in the dance. *(Degel mahane Efrayim)*[2]

A verse from the Torah, "All the people witnessed the thunder" (Exod. 20:15), occasioned this parable, which Moshe Hayyim Efrayim of Sedilikov related in the name of his grandfather, the Baal Shem Tov. Those words could also be read as "All the people saw the sounds," referring either to the blasts of the shofar at the moment of the Revelation at

145

Sinai or to the voice of God,[3] which was said to reverberate throughout
the world at that moment. Efrayim of Sedilikov connects that Torah verse
with a verse from Psalms,[4] which he interprets as follows: "Though the
Israelites present at that momentous moment of Revelation at Sinai were
unable to hear sounds, nevertheless from what they saw they were able to
grasp the deep and singular joy of that moment, and they made an
extraordinary effort to try to hear the sound and to understand the sweetness of the light of Torah." The homilist then contrasts the response of the
deaf man in the *mashal* with that of the Israelites in his own aggadic
depiction of the scene of Revelation.

Even without specific mention in the *nimshal*, the reader will probably
overhear in the above parable story a critique of the opponents of the
hasidic way, a critique of those who fail to hear the sweetness of the inner
melody that the Hasid hears and that moves him to dance. Dance as part
of the life of prayer and religious celebration is associated with Hasidism.
Its devotees would break out in dance, sometimes with great exuberance,
as an instinctive and natural way to express their joy and spiritual enthusiasm. Rabbi Nahman of Bratslav spoke of the joy of Torah study and of
the mitzvah that reaches the feet and moves them to break out in dance.[5]
The words of the psalmist—"All my bones shall say, 'Lord, who is like
You?'" (Ps. 35:10)—become very real as dance becomes a kind of prayerful activity—a form of prayer. The hasidic teachers, furthermore, considered dance to be a sacred act in which, like the words of a sacred text,
bodily motions symbolize sublime meanings.

Those unaffected and unmoved by the spirit of the emerging movement would direct criticism and even wrath upon the often joyous and
exuberant worship and celebration on the part of the followers of
Hasidism. The parable implicitly likens such critics to the deaf person
who both refuses to join the circle of dancers and is unable to understand
them. Like the deaf man in the parable, they too cannot hear the inner,
metaphorical music to which the Hasidim respond.

The spiritual experience to which the Hasid is open—the joy of God's
presence in all of life and the joy experienced in the presence of a holy
man whose whole being is bound up with the Divine—is likened to a
melody. Perhaps spiritual experience can best be understood in terms of
its parallel with the experience of music.

The parable assumes that the ecstatic response of a group of people to an inner experience testifies to its truth. The melody is heard, though not everyone can hear it, and the person unable to hear is then almost instinctively tempted to regard it as an illusion. Though the parable attributes to the deaf critic a lack of understanding, the reader might also detect a certain nuance not of denigration but rather of pity in the way the parable relates to the deaf person, suggesting the Hasid's pity for his opponents—those unable to grasp his own inner, spiritual experience.

---

1. Ecclesiastes 2:3.
2. *Degel mahane Efrayim* (1962), Yitro, p. 111.
3. See *Shemot rabbah*, 5:9.
4. Psalms 68:13. Exercising extreme liberty with the words of that difficult verse, several rabbinic sources (B. Shabbat 88b; *Mekhilta derabbi Yishma'el*, Yitro, Bahodesh, chap. 9; *Devarim rabbah*, 7:9; *Shir ha-shirim rabbah*, 8:11; and *Midrash tehillim,* 68:10) all connect that verse, in diverse ways, with the presence of angels at the Revelation scene.
5. *Likkute Moharan tinyana,* #81.

A Holy Man's Dependence upon His Followers

bird is perched at the very top of a tall tree beyond anyone's reach. However, if one person stands on the shoulders of another, and that person stands also on the shoulders of another, then the one standing on the very top is able to reach that bird. *(Degel maḥane Efrayim)*[1]

In another of his homilies found in the same volume,[2] Efrayim of Sedilikov wrote, "It is good that the people of Israel always be united in one fellowship, for then even those situated on a lower spiritual level assist their fellows to attain a greater level of holiness than would otherwise be possible. . . . *The person on a higher level has need for the person lower than himself,* and the person on a lower level has need for one higher than himself . . ." (italics added, AW). Without the support of others—even those on a lower spiritual level—one is incapable of the spiritual level one might otherwise attain.

In accentuating the holy man's dependence upon his community of followers, the above parable testifies to the contrast between eighteenth-century Hasidism and earlier stages of Jewish mysticism in which the mystic remained an isolated individual, not serving as a leader or center of any kind of human community. Gershom Scholem[3] defines the innovation of eighteenth-century Hasidism whereby the mystic—who is intrinsically turned inward and away from society—becomes at the same time the center of a community. The illumined—the person with the most profound inner life—is paradoxically the leader of a community. It is possible that the development in this direction began even prior to the

Baal Shem Tov and was found to a degree in the earlier years of the eighteenth century in the thinking and social patterns of various pietistic cells in Eastern European Jewry from which Hasidism emerged.[4]

It is only the holy man, not the others, who is able to reach for the bird perched at the top of the tree. In the implicit analogy, the clear distinction between holy man and follower remains and is in no way blurred. But importance, even crucial importance, is nonetheless assigned to the follower.

The comment of Efrayim of Sedilikov relates to a verse from the Torah in which Abraham "stood over them" (Gen. 18:8)—over the men (later understood to be angels) walking through the hot and inhospitable desert when Abraham ran to invite them to rest and to join him in a repast beneath a tree by his tent. The homilist understood Abraham's standing over his guests as his dependence upon them for the sake of his fulfilling his role, just as, in the parable, the man is able to reach for the bird only because he is standing upon those situated beneath him. To Efrayim of Sedilikov, the mention of Abraham's standing over his guests suggests the *tzaddik,* the holy man who can reach the bird at the highest point of the tree only because he stands upon the shoulders of others upon whom he is dependent. The exegesis in the homily perceives in the biblical patriarch Abraham a model of the hasidic holy man.

While the roles of *tzaddik* and Hasid—leader and follower—became actualized in terms of the social structure of the hasidic community only later, with the students of the Maggid of Mezherich (in what is termed the third generation of Hasidism), those respective roles came to be the distinguishing features of a hasidic community. The act of reaching for the bird, suggesting the holy man's more exalted level of mystic experience (the bird also serving as symbol for the Shekhinah) alludes to the role and capacity of the *tzaddik* upon whose higher spiritual level his followers are dependent. While his followers are not expected to attain anything like the level of the holy man around whom a hasidic community is constituted, an unusual interdependence nevertheless accompanies the dichotomy of the holy man and his followers.

The above parable was more fully developed in one of the legends of the Baal Shem Tov in which the Besht is praying with a number of his followers. While he prolongs his prayer due to the intensity of his praying, the others, having finished reciting their prayer, leave to attend to other matters. Later, when they reassemble, the Besht questions them and explains that while he was left alone, he could not continue to attain the same level of prayer as he could when they were praying together, for the power of his prayer is dependent upon his followers. And he relates to them a parable of a wondrously beautiful bird that migrated and perched itself at the top of a tall tree. The king desired that bird and gathered together a large contingent of men so that, standing one upon the other, the person on top might be able to reach the bird and obtain it for the king. Those below, however, did not hold those above them firmly enough, and as a consequence, the entire human ladder collapsed and the bird flew away.[5]

In connection with the parable as found in Degel maḥane Efrayim, its author, Efrayim of Sedilikov makes no mention of such a tradition relating to the Besht, his own grandfather. It would seem, therefore, that the legend developed later, the brief parable found in the Degel serving as the kernel of the later legend that reflects a crystallization of the tzaddik-Hasid relationship over time—a relationship that was then read back into the time of the Baal Shem Tov.[6]

1. Degel maḥane Efrayim (1962), p. 23, Va-era.
2. Ibid., p. 110, Yitro.
3. Gershom Scholem, Major Trends in Jewish Mysticism, p. 343.
4. See Ya'akov Hisdai, "Eved ha-Shem," pp. 253–292; and Mendel Piekarz, "Radikalizm dati bi-yemei reshit hitpashtut shel ha-ḥasidut be-aspeklariat kitve rabi Tzvi Hirsh mi-Galina," pp. 263–288.
5. Shelomo Gavriel Rosenthal, Hitgalut tzaddikim (1905), p. 28; ed. Gedalyah Nigal (1996), #7, pp. 38–40. The same legend is included in Midrash rivash tov (1927), p. 42; and in Martin Buber's Or ha-ganuz (1958), p. 76, quoting various earlier sources.
6. There is no evidence that the Baal Shem Tov was actually a leader of a group of followers in any formal sense; rather his circle appears to have consisted more of a group of peers—pneumatics without a recognized leader. The legendary history of the beginnings of Hasidism was written in a way to reflect the formation of communities around a holy man, with a sharp distinction between the tzaddik and his followers, a development that really unfolded in the generation of the students of the Maggid. Note Ada Rapoport-Albert's article, "Hasidism after 1772: Structural Continuity and Change," in Hasidism Reappraised, pp. 76–140.

Parables by Rabbi Nahman of Bratslav on Rabbi Nahman of Bratslav

❧

*T*here is a synagogue in Jerusalem where all the deceased of the world are brought, and immediately when a person dies he is brought there where he is judged to ascertain his location [in the hereafter]. For there is a place in the Land of Israel where they are brought up from outside the land and also vice versa. And there, in that synagogue, sits the court that judges every person and assigns to him the place he deserves. And there are those whom they judged who will not be given any place but are lost and hurled away as from a sling. And when a dead person is brought there, he is clad in garments [of the soul]. But one person might lack something of his garb; perhaps one might lack [the equivalent of] a glove or sleeve, and another might lack another part of his cloak, the hem, and the like, all according to the person's deeds, as is known. And according to his garments that are brought to him there, they judge him and assign him his place as mentioned above.

One time they brought there a dead person who was entirely naked without any garment at all, God forbid. And he was judged that he be cast off from one end of

151

the world to the other, God forbid, because he was entirely naked. But a *tzaddik* came and took a garment from among his very own garments and threw it over him. The court questioned the *tzaddik*, "Why are you giving him your own garment? For why is it that the dead person clads himself and is saved through a garment other than his own?" And they insisted upon an answer.

And to that the *tzaddik* answered, "I must send that person to a certain destination and for this reason I have permission to clad him in my garment. And have you not seen that at times an important official sends his servant to some other official, and the servant is detained for a time from going on his mission. When the first official asked him, "Why have you not yet set out on my mission?" the servant explained that he lacks a garment suitable for going to that other official. For the latter is an important person of rank and one cannot go there in a despicable garment. The minister answered, "Quickly, take one of my garments and wear it and run hurriedly to the official on my mission." And [the *tzaddik* explained] "since I need to send this deceased person on my mission, I am therefore giving him one of my own garments." And the *tzaddik* saved the dead person from the bitter punishment of being hurled from a bow.[1]

And he related this concerning the power of the true *tzaddik* to save his people in the world to come. (*Hayye Moharan, Sippurim hadashim)*[2]

The court sitting in judgment in a synagogue in Jerusalem resembles a rabbinic court—a *beit din*—which might have met in a synagogue of any Eastern European town. The listener imagines an extremely humble setting as the scene of the judgment. The particular nature of the judgment, however, adds to the scene an ambience of uncertainty and terror. And within that scene, already filled with anxiety, comes a naked man whose very nakedness assumes the dimensions of an infinite terror as the lack of spiritual garments leaves the soul to a destiny of restlessness and wandering without end.

The motif of the garments of the soul appears repeatedly in the Zohar. Each person through the course of his life weaves a garment of deeds for his soul. The soul always requires a garment. Just as in this world a soul needs a garment in the form of the body, so also following one's death the soul requires garments of a different nature, nonmaterial in character, woven of that person's mitzvot. The motif voices the utter terror of the soul's translation to another realm of being while failing to have the appropriate and needed garment, one composed of Torah learning and of holy deeds, in which to clad itself.[3] In the above parable, it is that state of intense shame and unbearable infliction that the *tzaddik* spares his follower.

The word *tzaddik*, which in earlier classical sources meant simply "righteous," acquired (especially within the milieu of mystic teaching and values) the sense of "holy man"—a person who has attained a high degree of spirituality and inner illumination. The term then came to be applied to the central figure and leader of a hasidic community—an alternative to the more traditional and conventional type of religious leadership that emphasized talmudic learning and erudition above all else. In Hasidism, the figure of the *tzaddik* is associated with inner depth and cleaving to God in every moment and aspect of life. It emphasized not the feats of the mind but rather those of the soul.

Rabbi Nahman of Bratslav, a great-grandson of the Baal Shem Tov, rebelled against much of the image and trappings of the *tzaddik* that had already developed in his time. As the leader of a flourishing hasidic community, the *tzaddik*'s court sometimes came to resemble, in some ways, a royal court. Penetrating beyond the external success of Hasidism, Rabbi

Nahman perceived the danger of an inner deterioration of the hasidic ethos, and in place of the more comfortable reliance upon the *tzaddik* and his spiritual attainment, he taught a much more intense and demanding mode of Hasidism. As noted earlier, he required, for example, that each of his followers devote an hour each day to personal, spontaneous prayer, having the character of soul-searching contemplation. He expected of every follower the agonizing spiritual searching that he himself knew.

In his brief lifetime (he died in 1810 at the age of thirty-eight), Rabbi Nahman never succeeded in attracting a significant number of followers, and among his followers a considerable number left him. Perhaps due to his own sense of failure he distinguished between *true tzaddikim* and others, implying that many of the leaders respected by large followings were not, in actuality, truly holy men.

From the unthinkable terror of his situation—one with no promise of parole—the man brought to the court is saved not simply by a *tzaddik* but by a *true tzaddik*. This story, which includes within it the parable of the minister and his servant, reveals both the extent of the power of Rabbi Nahman as a *true tzaddik,* and his infinite love for every one of his followers, even for the most undeserving.

This tale can be viewed as an exception against the background of the very sober temper typifying Bratslav Hasidism, which never preserved miracle tales in connection with Rabbi Nahman of the type that were frequently told by the followers of other rebbes.[4]

II

There is the person whose candle cannot remain lit for more than a very short time. During that time that the candle is lit he searches with it, but afterward the candle blows out and he has nothing with which to search. And there is one whose candle burns for a longer time span, and he has more time during which he may search, but afterward it too ceases. And there is the person whose candle burns for an entire day. And there are persons whose candle burns for longer and longer periods of time. But there is one who has many wondrous candles that burn and give light forever and are never extinguished. And that person is able to search endlessly among the concealed things in the royal chamber. He is indeed fortunate. *(Siḥot Haran)*[5]

The image of the candle in the parable represents a mitzvah (commandment, holy deed)—an association based on Proverbs 6:23, "For the mitzvah is a lamp; the Torah, a light. . . ." In the parable, a mitzvah creates a candle with which one may search among the many hidden things of the King in the world to come. It follows that according to a person's deeds in life, one is given a candle that burns for a certain period of time. Consequently, as explained in the *nimshal*, some can search only for a very limited time, but even during that time they merit finding wonderful things among the King's hidden objects; and the spiritual quality of one's life in the world to come parallels what he is able to find with the light of his candle. Others can search for a considerably longer time, making for a greater quality of life in the world to come. As the reader might detect, in the last sentence of the parable, Rabbi Nahman was referring to himself. "But the great *tzaddik*," it is related in the *nimshal*, "is allowed to search among the concealed things of the King for all time, and his candles will never become extinguished. . . ."

III

There was a king whose only son was very ill, and all the physicians ceased treating him, despairing of his recovery. At this same time one exceedingly wise physician came, and the king pleaded with him to make the attempt to heal his son. The physician answered honestly that, due to the nature of the illness, the chances for the son's recovery were remote. But, nevertheless, if they will follow one additional strategy it might then be possible to heal him. "But I don't know whether to inform you of this strategy for it is a very difficult one."

And when the king entreated him to reveal to him the strategy the physician was proposing, the latter told him, "Know that your son is so dangerously ill that it is no longer possible to place even a drop of medication in his mouth—medications that are extremely expensive even for just enough to fill a single small flask—and it is necessary to take large pails of such medicine to pour upon your sick son. Granted that all these expensive medications will be lost on him, nonetheless by this means his body will become strengthened ever so slightly, and perhaps by pouring upon him such a huge quantity of medication a drop or so will actually enter into his mouth. And through this means, it is possible that he will be healed." The king immediately concurred with this idea and ordered the treatment. And the prince was healed.

And the *nimshal* is readily understood: Insofar as we are so gravely ill, depressed with illness of the spirit, the *tzaddik* therefore needs to pour upon us precious and awesome medications. And even though it would seem that it all goes to waste, God forbid, nevertheless a good fragrance overcomes us and with time perhaps we will be able to absorb from the medicine some precious and awesome drop through our mouths and through our very innerness, until in this way there is hope for a complete healing. *(Shivḥe Moharan)*[6]

The parable story is a variation of a common folktale motif concerning one who heals the king's child of a seemingly hopeless disease.[7] The conventional forms of this motif typically involve some unusual (often magical) cure. However, the story line in Rabbi Nahman's parable is given a very rational tenor—no wonder cure is even suggested, only a recognition of the gravity of the illness and the ineffectiveness of the medication upon the patient. The healer makes no promises of recovery and prescribes what appears to be even a ludicrous treatment in the hope that it might perhaps have some positive effect in overcoming the disease. The story—substituting a realistic prognosis and prescription for a miraculous cure—can be seen to reflect the absence of wonder tales concerning Rabbi Nahman himself.

While the *mashal* avoids any diagnosis of the prince's disorder and presumably is speaking of a physical malady, the *nimshal* of this same parable refers to an illness of the spirit that is in need of healing. In that light, the parable is understood to refer to Rabbi Nahman himself as a healer of spiritual afflictions. His words and teachings are medication to effect a healing of the spirit. The parable conveys that while it is indeed probable that his words and teachings often have little effect upon his followers, there is the possibility, even if remote, that any particular word, any inventive twist of thought, any expression in his teaching or stories might bring spiritual healing to the person so afflicted. That healing is equivalent to *teshuvah*, to a true turning to God, a turning away from self and from material strivings.

A shift occurs in the transition between the parable story and the stated application. The listener at first identifies with the king who is concerned with his son's illness. The *nimshal,* however, effects a different identification as the listener comes to view himself as the sick child in need of healing. Just as a realization of one's physical illness can be the first step in the process of healing, so a realization of one's spiritual disorder is the initial step on the way to a healing of the spirit.

In its attempt to explain the profusion of the master's *torot* (teachings; lectures), one might seek alternative explanations for Nahman's wordy and extremely complicated teachings. Though the hasidic master was obviously concerned with communication—with presenting his thoughts in a way that would speak to his followers—at the same time the function of the hasidic homily might also extend beyond that concern for communication. The hasidic homily is also an opportunity for the master to clarify his own thinking, and in a certain sense those listening to the homily were overhearing the master's thinking to himself as he developed his own nuanced worldview and interpretation of basic hasidic concepts. This suggestion might be particularly applicable to the very complex *torot* of Rabbi Nahman.

---

1. The expression is based on I Samuel 25:29.
2. *Hayye Moharan, Sippurim hadashim* (1961), #22, pp. 24b–25a.
3. Gershom Scholem, *"Levush ha-neshamot ve-haluka derabanan,"* pp. 290–306.
4. Arthur Green, *Tormented Master,* pp. 9, 14.
5. *Sihot Haran,* #134, included in *Shivhe Haran* (1961), p. 91.
6. *Shivhe Moharan, Ma'alot torato ve-sippurav ha-kedoshim,* #51, pp. 16b–17a, included in *Hayye Moharan* (1962).
7. Stith Thompson, *Motif-Index of Folk-Literature,* F950 (Marvelous cures), F950.8 (Princess cured by seeing her lover dance), T67.2 (Marriage to prince as reward for curing him); Antti Aarne, *The Types of the Folktale,* #460, #461, #610–619. In two of the famous Tales of Rabbi Nahman, the reader hears echoes of the motif of a king seeking a cure for his ailing son or daughter: in the fifth Tale ("The King Who Had No Children") and in the account of the sixth day in the last of his Tales ("The Seven Beggars"). Note also the parable in *Sha'ar ha-melekh* by Mordecai ben Shmuel of Vilkatsh, p. 562.

To Break Down All the Doors and Locks

⤳

Every lock has a key that opens and fits that particular lock, but there are also thieves who open doors and locks without using any key at all but rather by simply breaking the lock. Similarly, every hidden matter has a key, namely the *kavvanah,* the specific contemplation appropriate to that matter. But the ideal key is to do as the thief does and break down everything, namely break one's own heart with submission, thus breaking the barrier separating man from God, which serves as the lock keeping man out. *(Keter shem tov)*[1]

This parable is included in *Keter shem tov* by Aharon ben Meir ha-kohen of Apt, who related it in the name of Rabbi Baer—most likely Dov Baer of Mezherich—whose teachings are frequently included in that work by Aharon of Apt. The following version of the above analogy is found in a homily by Binyamin of Zalozetz, who ascribed the parable to the Maggid of Mezherich.

> It sometimes happens that people open a lock with a key, but there is also the case of a person who has no key and who needs to break the door and the lock with some strong object capable of breaking iron. So it is that the earlier generations, after the destruction of the Temple,

159

would open all the locked gates with keys, namely, the *kavvanot*. The later generations, however, lack the power of the *kavvanot* and consequently we must break all the locks without keys, employing instead simply the shattering of our own evil hearts. . . . *(Turei zahav)*[2]

In a collection of hasidic stories from a later period,[3] the above parable is ascribed to the Baal Shem Tov, the central figure in the emergence of Hasidism, after he himself, to prove his point, took the paper upon which was written the specific *kavvanah* to be recited prior to the sounding of the shofar on Rosh Hashanah. The person appointed to sound the shofar and unable to locate the written *kavvanah* would be in a state of dismay. And that situation would occasion the parable related by the Baal Shem Tov, which questions the need for such *kavvanot*. This would appear to be another example of a parable that, over time, served as the kernel of a legend told concerning the Baal Shem Tov.

Hasidism claimed as a fundamental part of its legacy the body of mystic teaching associated with Rabbi Isaac Luria (1534–1572), even though hasidic teaching in some significant ways followed a different spiritual and ideological direction than the teachings of Lurianic Kabbalah.[4] Although not without a measure of ambivalence in certain of its circles, Hasidism made an open break with a Lurianic practice which, in time, became more and more complicated, with the reciting of *kavvanot*—designated statements to be recited with contemplation prior to performing certain mitzvot. The *kavvanot* were believed to enhance the effectiveness of those acts in restoring the Divine Unity. Hasidism ceased the practice of the *kavvanot*, it would seem, because they required a degree of mental activity that could only impede *devekut*—a complete mental attachment to God. The complexity and intricacy of those *kavvanot* came to seem quite irrelevant to the prayerful soul.[5]

The parable both testifies to and attempts to explain that break with the practice of reciting the *kavvanot*, which are found in various kabbalistic prayer books. The image in the parable is related to Psalms 51:19, "True sacrifice to God is a contrite spirit; God, You will not despise a contrite and crushed heart." In the light of that connection, the act of the thief who, without keys, simply breaks down the door, becomes analogous to the person with a broken heart who, in true regret and contrition, is no longer in need of what the Hasid views as artificial keys in the form of *kavvanot*. The parable voices the theme of decline through time in its explanation that earlier generations were capable of thinking of the *kavvanah* (thus exercising a cognitive function) without interfering at the same time with the demands of prayerfulness—a combination that later generations were unable to juggle. For contemporaries, the mind and soul cannot both work together, and attention to the *kavvanah* came to be considered a hindrance to the state of being appropriate to performing a holy deed.[6]

The parable's impact flows from the decidedly unexpected choice of a thief as a model of determined will. The criminal who, with unqualified intent, does not rely on keys but simply breaks down the door represents the person of true piety in coming before God with humility and contrition. While the art of parable often likens an act or situation in one sphere of life to that of a very contrasting sphere of life, in this case the parable establishes a parallel between a presumably moral universe and a decidedly immoral world. The juxtaposition makes for a striking and powerful parable.

---

1. *Keter shem tov* (1868), 16a.
2. *Turei zahav* (1989), p. 151.
3. *Or yesharim* (1924), 52b.
4. See Berakha Zack, "Rabbi Moshe Cordovero's Influence upon Hasidism," pp. 229–246; and Moshe Idel, *Hasidism*, pp. 160–161, 215, 235. Both point to the greater affinity of Hasidism with the mystic teachings of Cordovero with their greater emphasis upon divine immanence.
5. See Arthur Green, "Hasidism: Discovery and Retreat," p. 110.
6. See Rivka Schatz Uffenheimer, *Hasidism as Mysticism*, pp. 215–241.

Which Class Really Makes the Wheels Go Around?

I once heard, from my grandfather, a parable of a king who engaged in war. He had many foot soldiers and also horsemen. And in war the foot soldiers would stand bound one to another with iron rings so that they could not move from their places; unable to flee in any direction, they stood firm in the thick of battle. When the horsemen felt the real thick of the fighting, though they too were in war, they would flee with their horses and not risk their lives, unlike the foot soldiers who would sacrifice their lives in war for the glory of the king.

And after the Lord helped their side to triumph in war, the horsemen would then come and seize the booty that their horses were able to carry away. But the foot soldiers took nothing at all except a little bread and water to revive their lives a day at a time, for the booty was too heavy for them to carry, and they were content simply that they emerged from the struggle alive.

And since we all serve one king for the sake of his exalted glory, we have trust that when the war is over, if I will lack something, the horsemen will give me what I need. For we serve one king, and it stands to reason that we deserve a portion of that booty even more than the horsemen do, for with God's help we brought about the king's victory at the risk of our lives, while they do not risk their lives. They refuse, however, to share their spoils with the foot soldiers, even so much as food for a single meal, claiming that they achieved the victory. (*Degel maḥane Efrayim*)[1]

Though the meaning of the above parable itself might be quite transparent, Rabbi Efrayim of Sedilikov nevertheless explains that the two types, the foot soldiers and the horsemen, represent respectively *anshe tzurah* (people of spirit and mind) and *anshe homer* (people of material bent and means).[2] The former are materially disadvantaged and dependent upon the *anshe homer*, who do not respond to their needs even though in reality the *anshe tzurah* are the real soldiers in life.

While one might assume that the horsemen occupy a higher level in the military hierarchy, the parable paradoxically alters and shatters that evaluation. Society's conventional evaluation of its various sectors can err as those given honor, prestige, and credit are not necessarily those actually responsible for real accomplishment. That accomplishment, in truth—as becomes clear to the reader—belongs to the *anshe tzurah* because they have an innate sense of commitment and it is contrary to their nature to retreat from the battle. Those who tend the pastures of worldly wealth are, in truth, dependent upon those devoted to the pursuits of mind and spirit.

In the light of this parable, the material wealth in the hands of the more material-minded class is really of the nature of booty and hence is of questionable legitimacy. It is not really theirs but rather belongs, with greater justification, to the *anshe tzurah*, with whom the hasidic teacher identifies himself, as is evidenced by the sudden transition to the first person in the parable.

Referring to a talmudic expression, "when earth and heaven kiss,"[3] Efrayim of Sedilikov understood "earth" and "heaven" to suggest, respectively, *anshe homer* and *anshe tzurah* who, ideally, should cooperate for the good of both. And when cooperation and justice prevail here below, this effects a just state in the higher worlds as well. The homilist looks at society and at the world through the lens of the learned class, which he himself represents, and it is clear in his mind that the pursuits and contribution of the world of trade and economic endeavor are but a means to the higher values to which he himself subscribes.

The nuance of bitterness in this parable serves as a window to social tensions within eighteenth-century Eastern European Jewish society and reflects the material distress of some of the spiritual guides of eighteenth-century Jewry. Some historians have perceived in that background a major factor in the emergence of Hasidism, although today it would be considered inaccurate to interpret Hasidism as a movement of social protest, drawing its supporters exclusively from an economically disenfranchised population. The historical evidence now suggests rather that Hasidism attracted Jews from various socioeconomic strata. The parable could more realistically voice the claim that the followers, often in more comfortable economic circumstances, are actually dependent upon the *tzaddik* and upon his power and influence in the higher worlds affecting this lower world. They consequently owe him material support, a position expressed with unmistakable emphasis in the homilies of Elimelekh of Lyzhansk, a student of the Maggid of Mezherich. Perhaps the parable more likely reflects the personal economic condition of Efrayim of Sedilikov himself who, despite his status as a grandson of the Baal Shem Tov, had few followers and (unlike his affluent brother, Baruch of Mezebov) lived in extremely modest circumstances.[4]

1. *Degel mahane Efrayim* (1963), p. 155, Tzav.
2. The two expressions mean "people of form" and "people of matter," a polarity ultimately going back to Aristotle's metaphysical differentiation between form and matter, reaching Hasidism through medieval Jewish philosophy.
3. B. Baba Batra 74a.
4. Simon Dubnow, *Toledot ha-hasidut*, pp. 204–208.

More Treasure Tales

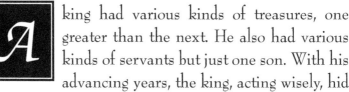

king had various kinds of treasures, one greater than the next. He also had various kinds of servants but just one son. With his advancing years, the king, acting wisely, hid important treasures in a structure within the walls of the royal chamber. He made a single, slight alteration in the wall that might be detected by a wise person. And in that concealed location, marked by no more than a minute, subtle indication, he would place his more important treasures. Afterward he told his son all that he had done and added, "Know that all that I have done makes sense, so make an effort to understand."

After the king's death, the servants grabbed the evident, revealed treasures, while the son instead made the effort to understand what his father had told him, and following careful consideration and investigation he sensed something different about the wall in that particular place. He searched, aided by that subtle alteration in the wall, and found a treasure. And afterward he considered further and realized that the subtle alteration was also a sign that an even more important treasure could be found. *(Toledot Ya'akov Yosef)* [1]

Our collection of hasidic parables opened with a parable about a treasure. Nearing the end of our journey, we return to that same subject as it appears in other parables told by the hasidic masters.

While quite a number of the parables we have read seek to illuminate differences between the spirituality of Hasidism and the non-hasidic Jewish world, the following parables—which both refer to a kind of archaeology concerning the burying and discovery of treasure—focus, instead, on the differences between the Jewish teaching and legacy and the cultural inheritance of the larger world surrounding Jewry. More precisely, the following two parables distinguish between the wisdom of Israel and that of the other nations of the world and seek to clarify the difference between them.

In the homily of Rabbi Ya'akov Yosef of Polonnoye, a situation is described that occasions the parable, and the question is posed: Why are the Seven Wisdoms (the basic areas of knowledge) not found in the Talmud, the classic repository of Jewish law, tradition, and wisdom?

In his homily containing this parable, Rabbi Ya'akov Yosef explains the parable as comparing more external types of wisdom, which the nations of the world more easily discover, with a deeper and more precious type of wisdom that is not nearly so easily discoverable. The latter kind of wisdom is of a different character and quality and, unlike the more evident treasures, is comprised of the awe of God, inlaid with love.

One overhears in the background of the parable an implied claim that the types of knowledge and wisdom possessed by the Western world greatly exceed, if not perhaps render irrelevant, the type of wisdom associated with Jewish tradition and teaching and with the traditions of Jewish mysticism in particular. At the time that the above parable was composed, Western culture had not yet had any decisive impact upon Eastern European Jewry and the two cultural worlds seemed ever so distant one from the other. Jews in Eastern Europe nevertheless did have a very general awareness of Western knowledge. In the eighteenth century, Western culture assumed a distinctly rationalist direction, and although modern science was still at a relatively early stage in its development, an emphatic focus on the empirical cast doubt upon anything beyond the range of the senses and the analysis of sensual, empirical knowledge. In this parable, Rabbi Ya'akov Yosef responds to that challenge with a counterclaim that the secular, external wisdom—including such knowledge as the mathematics and science of the time—is more accessible to the human mind and to the world at large for the reason that it is of lesser depth and lesser ultimate value. If the entire universe is a garment in which the Divine is clad, empirical science and its culture were content with exploring the garment; a deeper kind of wisdom is required to perceive the presence of God concealed within that garment.

Significant in the parable is the contrast between the king's servants and his son. The servants grab hold of the treasures closer to the surface of the ground, those more easily discernible, suggesting the revealed (and external) forms of wisdom. The son, in contrast, acting upon an allusion heard within his father's advice to him, digs deeper and seeks the more precious treasure that is buried at a deeper and hence less accessible level within the ground.

The son, clearly suggesting the people Israel, digs beyond the level at which others dug and finds the awe of God—a wisdom with a character of devoutness; and still deeper he locates that treasure that is inlaid with love, an "inner treasure," one of greater depth and one presumably found within the self.[2]

Within the discussion comprising the *nimshal,* the highest good is identified as *devekut,* an inner attachment to the Divine, which, in hasidic teaching, is the goal of all aspects of religious life. The reader cannot overlook the fact that the deeper wisdom found in the story is defined precisely in terms of the hasidic ideal of *devekut.* The parable story exalts the spiritual legacy of the Jewish people, which is incomprehensible and unappreciated by the culture and science of the larger non-Jewish world. But the parable, as explained, also reveals the Hasid's exalted valuation of his own ideology within the panorama of traditional Jewry.

With historical hindsight, this parable might be seen to acquire additional significance at a later stage of Hasidism when, during the course of the nineteenth century, it had attained a position of influence and, in many places, dominance in traditional Jewish society in Eastern Europe. In that later stage, Hasidism identified completely with traditional Jewish society against the growing challenge of Haskalah, the movement of enlightenment and modernization. Haskalah insisted, first and foremost, upon creating a window to the European cultural world—its knowledge and its values—including the sciences, which were likened in Ya'akov Yosef's parable to the lesser treasures placed within proximity of the surface. In its opposition to secular learning, Hasidism situated itself within the camp ultimately identified today as *haredi*—the ultra-traditional Jewish population that considers the pursuit of secular learning and the energies placed in that direction as threatening to the life and study of Torah. While Hasidism emerged on the scene of history as a pietistic transformation of Jewish tradition from within, its later conflict with Haskalah and its growing perception of modern Western culture as foreign to its values largely transformed Hasidism into a fortress directed against modernity itself.[3]

A somewhat similar parable, also concerning precious treasure buried within the ground, is included in *Or ha-emet,* a text containing teachings of the Maggid of Mezherich, though this parable was admittedly added by the editor of the collection who specified that the passages toward the end of the collection, including this parable, are not the words of "our master."

II

A king dug places to hide good wine within the ground at several locations and in several chambers, and he placed superior wine in a still deeper room, and he placed his treasures and hidden things at a still deeper level far beneath all the chambers. And he announced that anyone who can make his way to any of the rooms may take wine for himself and bring some of the wine to the king, the king's intent being simply to ascertain the diligence of the servants. He announced a reward for that person who would bring some of the better wine placed in a deeper chamber; moreover he announced that the person who is still more diligent and would reach that still deeper level of the treasures beneath all the chambers may take whatever his heart desires.

Now one group entered only into a chamber of the uppermost level, for when they sought to enter into a deeper chamber, their candles blew out due to the boiling effect of the wine, and they brought to the king only from the wine on that higher level. And noting their laziness, the king despised them. A second group acted with greater skill and strategy, bringing with them more candles; they were able to enter into the second chamber, but the candles were of no help when it came to entering into the third chamber. The third group, taking with them candles of greater thickness, arrived at the third chamber but were unable to enter. But there were some wise men among them who made thick candles and torches that would not easily be extinguished. But prior to their coming to the chamber where the treasures had been placed, the candles [and even the torches] began to blow out. What did they do? They consulted with one another and agreed that they would remove their clothes and ignite them, for they realized that should they come to the chamber of the treasures they would take whatever their hearts desire. Their plan succeeded, and they took whatever they desired from the hidden chamber. They took also precious stones to provide light for their return. And the king greatly rejoiced in their diligence. *(Or ha-emet)*[4]

The image of wine, serving as an attraction to the king's servants, connotes inner richness and also a variance of quality.[5] Not all wine is of the same quality. Like the parable related by Rabbi Ya'akov Yosef above, there is an archaeological context: the more precious treasure is found buried at a deeper level within the earth. The parable story is of the nature of a test, as the king devises a way to measure the diligence of his servants. It is meritorious for a servant to exert an effort and use ingenuity to find the more hidden treasure, even though his discovery of the treasure is not for the king's benefit but for his own. While in the parable story the king gives a reward for the one who makes the greater effort and brings the more precious treasure, the implied *nimshal* would convey that those articles placed at greater depth and hence more inaccessible are reward in themselves; the treasure is its own reward.

This *mashal* contains the familiar triad so basic to the folktale. Here the triad concerns three groups of servants. Even those of the third group, although making efforts beyond those of the two preceding groups, fail twice in their goal until they take the final step and disrobe in order to use their clothes to produce the greater fire necessary to be able to see in the darkness. The reader might ask whether the act of removing clothing alludes to the removing of the ego—their sense of self—as they attain a level of *ayin*, removing all self-interest and awareness of self as a prerequisite to the mystic quest of union with the Divine.

The *mashal* concludes on a note of the king's rejoicing, suggesting that it is God's will that man engage in a spiritual quest for depth of understanding. The homily text identifies the fulfillment of this quest with *devekut*—again the hasidic ideal of the person's total, inner attachment to the Divine. That goal, the apex of the worship of God, requires "desire, delight, and enthusiasm." In light of the parable, it is understood that the way of *devekut* is not simple, but requires pronounced diligence, reaching far beyond conventional norms.

---

1. *Toledot Ya'akov Yosef* (1973), Be-har, 1:423, related in the name of the *Moharaz*.
2. Ibid., 1:424.
3. One might suggest that the phenomenon of present-day followers of hasidic movements divorced from secular learning, either entirely or relating to it with decided qualification, ignores certain insights found in hasidic texts themselves. Since the totality of being is interwoven with Torah, in one important sense Torah is found everywhere, within all that exists. Torah, ultimately, is not limited to particular texts, but includes all knowledge. Note for example, the comments of a later hasidic teacher in *Sefat emet* of Yehudah Aryeh Lev of Gur, V, Parshat Devarim, homilies dated 1901–1903 (English translation by Arthur Green, p. 285).

4. *Or ha-emet* (1899), 106ab.

5. In a parable included in *Ḥayye Moharan, Gedulat hasagato* #20, Rabbi Nahman of Bratslav likens himself to the choicest wine in comparison with other *tzaddikim*: "They [other hasidic communities] will never be able to mislead us, for we have tasted the good wine, etc."

Where the True Treasure
Is to Be Found

~

henever a young man would journey for the very first time to the *tzaddik* [the hasidic holy man] to visit his court, Rabbi Bunam would tell him that he should know what occurred in the case of Reb Izik [the son of] Reb Yekelish of Krakow, who built the synagogue in Krakow known as Reb Izik Reb Yekelish's *shul*. And this is what took place:

Reb Izik R. Yekelish dreamed a number of times that he should journey to Prague, and there, adjacent to the king's palace beneath the bridge, he should dig in the ground where he would find a great treasure and would become rich. So he journeyed to Prague, and upon arriving he approached the bridge near the royal palace. But soldiers were walking on patrol there day and night, and he feared to proceed to dig in the ground in quest of hidden things. He was greatly distressed, for after having gone to such tremendous effort he would be returning home with nothing. All day long he would walk back and forth near the bridge, preoccupied with his thoughts, and when it became dark, he would return to the inn to rest. Again the next day and the day following, he would come in the morning to that same place and he would walk around there all day long, and toward evening he would return again to the inn. Day after day, the official standing there, the head of the king's guards, would see a Jew who looked like a poor man clad in sadness and distress, walking around and around near the bridge. So he called out to him and, in a gentle way, asked him, "What are you looking for, for whom are you waiting here all these days?" So he told [the guard] all that had happened, that several nights in succession he had a dream that here a great treasure is buried, and for this purpose he came, with great effort and trouble, to Prague. And then the official broke out laughing and he remarked to him, "Was it worth journeying such a long way simply because of a dream? Who believes in dreams anyway? I myself had a dream in which I was told to journey to the city of Krakow where there is a certain person named Izik R. Yekelish, and that if I dig there beneath his stove, in the house of that Jew, Izik R. Yekelish, I would find a great treasure. But do you think I would trust in empty dreams? And for this purpose to journey to Krakow? And in coming here, you did just that sort of foolishness!"

Now, when Izik R. Yekelish heard the official's words, he understood that the real purpose of his coming here was that he might hear those words and know that the treasure is not found here but rather in his very own house, that he must dig and seek within his own dwelling and there he will find the treasure. He turned around and journeyed home and he searched and found the treasure in his house beneath the stove. And with its wealth, he built the synagogue named after him.

Similarly, each young man coming to the *tzaddik*, to the *rebbe*, should know that the treasure is not to be sought at the home of the *rebbe* but rather within his own home and that there he should seek and dig as deeply as he is able, and if you make the effort you will find it. Realize and understand that "the thing is very close to you, in your mouth and in your heart, to observe it" (Deut. 30:14)—truly where one is. *(Sefer simḥat Yisra'el)*[1]

We conclude, as we began, with a parable about a treasure, this time with a passage suggesting that each person is a treasure, that each has a unique treasure in one's own inner life and must seek that spiritual treasure precisely within the self.

The late Dov Sadan[2] pointed out that Izik the son of Yekelish was actually an historical figure who, over time, became the subject of folk sayings. Unlike what is told in the story, the historical Izik ben Yekelish was born into great wealth. He held a high position within the Jewish community of Krakow where he built a synagogue.

The institution of the organized hasidic community under the leadership of a holy man (*tzaddik*) contributed to the rapid spread of Hasidism through a considerable part of Eastern European Jewry. The role of the *tzaddik* or *rebbe* acquired a central place in hasidic life and teaching, both in the eyes of its followers and in the eyes of its opponents. For many of its followers, the holy man, the mystic, at the center of any particular hasidic community was thought to be a connection with God, a bridge to the Divine. As mentioned previously, the Maggid of Mezherich, whose students generally became the central figures of the communities that they established in different localities, defined the role of the hasidic holy man as eliciting *ayin* from *yesh*, countering the emergence of corporeal being out of the hidden mystery of the Divine.[3] To the opponents of Hasidism, the social organization of the hasidic community centered around the *tzaddik*—an alternative to the traditional Jewish community with its official institutions and leadership—provoked both apprehension and hostility.[4] It was felt that the holy man took the place of the Torah itself as the center of Jewish existence.

The role of the *tzaddik*, personifying the ethos of the hasidic teaching, included that possibility. Outward conformity to the practices and distinguishing features of a particular hasidic community—more precisely conformity to the particular practices and traits of a certain *rebbe*—could also overshadow the master's own spiritual teaching. With the flourishing of the movement in large parts of Eastern Europe, adherence to a hasidic court became fashionable and the adherence to a *tzaddik* could easily substitute for the follower's own pursuit of a spiritual path. In this way, the flourishing of Hasidism and of hasidic communities contained the seed of potential spiritual superficiality.

With the spread of Hasidism and its institutional success, Simhah Bunam of Pryzucha—himself a hasidic *rebbe*—felt that the hasidic reality had too often betrayed what he considered to be the very essence of the hasidic idea.[5] Like Rabbi Nahman of Bratslav and like Menahem Mendel of Kotsk (one of Simhah Bunam's own disciples), Simhah Bunam raised his voice against the lavish trappings of the affluent hasidic court. He disapproved of its low intellectual level and its frequent emphasis upon the *tzaddik* as a wonder-worker. Turning to the *tzaddik* and becoming a member of a hasidic community could become, for all too many, an end in itself rather than a means to the follower's own personal spiritual quest and development. It was in this general context of superficiality and degeneration, and especially a shallow imitation of and identification with the *rebbe*, that Simhah Bunam, the rebel *rebbe* in early nineteenth-century Poland, would relate his parable to the young men drawn to his court to become his followers. Simhah Bunam might rightly be described as both *rebbe* and anti-*rebbe* at the same time.

In broader perspective, the complaint heard in Simhah Bunam's parable is related also to the tendency, present from the beginning, to place significantly greater emphasis upon the holy man as a person capable of fulfilling the goal of *devekut* in its various ramifications, while others, it was assumed, were able to walk in that path to a much more minimal extent. Their measure of *devekut* came to acquire the form of cleaving to the *tzaddik* rather than in spiritual striving and efforts on their own part. The more creative nuances voiced in some of the parables and in hasidic teaching were regarded as relevant only to the *tzaddik*, whereas the path for the multitude of followers was defined solely in terms of the traditional corpus of talmudic study, prayer, and the mitzvot—which Hasidism shared also with its critics. The Hasid's response to God's Presence was to be expressed in those accepted and conventional ways and in those ways only.[6] The role of the Hasid became first and foremost that of being a follower. Against this background one can understand the hasidic voice of protest in the above parable attributed to Rabbi Simhah Bunam.

A variation of the same story is found in one of the later Bratslav texts—*Kokhve or*[7]—within a group of stories that generally lack the idiom and unique character of the stories associated with Rabbi Nahman. (We note that in a more recent edition of the same text those stories are deleted altogether.)[8] The story in that Bratslav source differs from Simhah Bunam's account in that the central figure in the story is nameless and he has his dream only once. As in the story related by Rabbi Simhah Bunam, the Bratslav version is similarly told as an occurrence that actually happened and is followed by a *nimshal*. In *Kokhve or*, the application is stated as follows: "And so it is [also] with the divine worship [*avodah*], that the treasure is near each person, within his very self, but to know of the treasure it is necessary to journey to the *tzaddik*."

Dov Sadan pointed out that the narrative motif of this tale was prevalent among Central European folktales but without the kind of ideological thrust present in the hasidic story.[9] It would appear that Rabbi Simhah Bunam utilized a well-known narrative strand of one's seeking something far away when it is actually to be found in his own location,[10] providing that folk motif with an ideological implication.

It is interesting to note, however, that the same basic story, with change of place names—Baghdad and Cairo in place of Krakow and Prague—is found in a poetic work of the medieval Persian Sufi poet, Jalal al-Din Rumi[11] who lived some five hundred years prior to the emergence of eighteenth-century Hasidism.

The very context of Rumi's poetry—its symbolism and core spiritual meaning—provides for the tale an implied ideological dimension: that each person must look into himself, into his own innerness and soul, for the real treasure. Without making the claim for a direct path leading from a much earlier Sufi tale from a very different geographical and cultural area to the story related by an early nineteenth-century hasidic master in Poland, the similarity between the two stories might serve as a sign of broader, non-textual parallels between Hasidism and Sufism in their theological emphases and mystic insights; in their attempt to renew and transform a religious tradition from within; and in the historical fate of Hasidism and Sufism which, over time, also suffered the effects of institutionalization.[12] Going further, it might buttress the sense that a more complete grasp of the historical phenomenon of Hasidism must seriously consider the impact, though indirect, of the medieval mystic Islamic school of Sufism upon Hasidism, which arose several centuries later.[13]

The above parable of Simhah Bunam points to one of the many tensions found within Hasidism and hasidic teaching. As important as the *tzaddik*'s role in Hasidism came to be, and as much as Hasidism came to identify itself in terms of the hasidic holy man, that very institution and role may have distanced Hasidism from certain insights present within its own teaching. For example, in reference to God's promise to Abraham that his descendents would be as numerous as the stars of the heavens (Gen. 15:5), Rabbi Kalonymus Kalman Epstein commented that the particular parallel with the stars was chosen for the reason that a star shines by its own light![14]

---

1. *Sefer simḥat Yisra'el* (1981), 47a.
2. Dov Sadan, *"Ha-otzar: le-darko shel mashal ve-nimshal,"* pp. 117–118.
3. *Maggid devarav le-Ya'akov* (1976), #190. See also Arthur Green, "The *Zaddik* as *Axis Mundi* in Later Judaism," pp. 327–347.
4. Note Mendel Piekarz, *Bi-yeme tzemiḥat ha-ḥasidut,* in which the author presents the claim that the opposition and hostility to Hasidism arose not because of its ideas, which were found also in older sources and in older strata of Eastern European Jewish thought, but rather because of its comprising an alternative Jewish community.
5. See Raphael Mahler, *Hasidism and the Jewish Enlightenment,* pp. 267–303, on the schools of Pryzucha and Kotsk and their differences from contrasting schools within Polish Hasidism.

6. Miles Krassen, *Uniter of Heaven and Earth,* especially pp. 184–186; 193; 212–214. In addition to a more realistic view concerning the general potential of a population to attain *devekut,* this direction might also be seen, in part, as an impact of the persecution of the Hasidim at the hands of their critics and their fear of continued hostility should they relate seriously to the more radical nuances in their own teaching.

7. *Kokhve or,* ed. Avraham Hazan (1961), *Ma'asiyot u-meshalim,* p. 26.

8. *Kokhve or* (1987).

9. Dov Sadan in "*Ha-otzar,*" pp. 116–124.

10. Antti Aarne, *The Types of the Folktale,* Type 1645 (The treasure at home); Stith Thompson, *Motif-Index of Folk-Literature,* N531 (Treasure discovered through dream); N531.1 (Dream of treasure on bridge). Note the sources referred to in connection with the above motifs and tale types including references to Arabic tales.

11. Jalal al-Din Rumi, *More Tales from the Masnavi,* #197.

12. Note in particular, Annemarie Schimmel, *Mystic Dimensions of Islam,* p. 343; also Stephen Pastner and Rhonda Berger-Sofer, "*Rebbe* and *Pir.*"

13. The impact of Sufism upon Hasidism revolves around the mystic teachings of Moses Cordovero of sixteenth-century Safed, a most significant influence upon hasidic thought via his impact upon writers of the kabbalistic ethical literature such as Moshe deVidash and Yishayahu Horowitz. (Note Berakha Zack, "Rabbi Moshe Cordovero's Influence upon Hasidism"; also Paul Fenton, ed. and trans., *The Treatise of the Pool,* pp. 63–64; and Moshe Idel, *Hasidism: Between Ecstasy and Magic.*) Cordovero was himself influenced by Abraham Abulafia and Yitzhak ben Shmuel of Acre, both of whom exemplified Sufi influence directly or indirectly (Adolf Yellinek, *Beitraege zur Geschichte der Kabbala*). Significant signs of the proximity and influence of Islamic mysticism upon the very scene of the renaissance of kabbalistic teaching in Safed in the sixteenth century have been noted (Joseph Yanon, "*Hashpa'ot tzufiot al ha-kabbalah be-Tzefat*"). The kabbalistic writings produced or inspired by the revival of mystic thought in Safed of that period comprised, to a large degree, the intellectual and spiritual soil in which eighteenth-century Hasidism developed. Together these indications suggest that Hasidism emerged in the spiritual shadow of concepts and of the kind of spiritual awareness that typified Islamic mysticism at a significantly earlier point in time. See Gershom Scholem, "A Note on a Kabbalistical Treatise on Contemplation"; Paul Fenton, ed. and trans., *The Treatise of the Pool,* p. 63; and Efrayim Gottlieb, "*Devekut* and Prophecy in *Otzar ha-hayyim.*"

14. *Ma'or va-shemesh,* pp. 87–88, Lekh Lekha.

Glossary of Terms and Personalities

acosmic—a worldview in which, ultimately, God is the only reality.

ayin—"nothingness," but only in the sense of being noncorporeal and hence a nonentity only from a physical criterion in terms of what can be known through the senses and measured and investigated empirically. From a higher perspective, *ayin* is the most real. Corporeality, however, acquires its (relative) reality only through the presence of the *ayin* within it and underlying it.

Baal Shem Tov—the "Master of the Good Name," Yisra'el ben Eliezer, the central figure in early Hasidism. He died in Mezebov in 1760. Though he left virtually no writings, he is quoted extensively in hasidic texts that appeared after his lifetime.

Beit Hillel—the students of Hillel, a sage who taught in Jerusalem during the latter part of the first century B.C.E. In talmudic law, the traditions and legal decisions of Beit Hillel were, in most cases, accepted over those of its rival school, Beit Shammai.

Beit Shammai—the students of Shammai, a contemporary of Hillel.

Besht—acronym for the Baal Shem Tov.

contraction—see *tzimtzum*.

Cordovero, Moshe—a leading kabbalistic thinker who, through important kabbalistic ethical works that his teaching inspired, was a major influence upon hasidic thought. He died in Safed in 1570.

devekut—an uninterrupted, inner awareness and mental attachment to God; the major goal of hasidic spirituality.

Divine Wisdom—the higher transcendent state of the Torah, which is one with God.

ecstatics—mystics who experience intense ecstasy and display signs of ecstatic enthusiasm in their behavior.

Ein Sof—the completely unbounded, undefined, formless, and infinite state of the Divine, beyond the reach of human thought or language.

Evil Inclination—the rabbinic concept of a natural propensity within each human being for selfishness, evil, ego, and material striving. The Evil Inclination is coupled with a Good Inclination, the cultivation of which requires education and character training.

Giving of the Torah—the rabbinic concept of the Revelation; the scene of the Revelation at Sinai, which included the giving of both the written and oral teachings to Moses and Israel, as well as all later interpretations of the Torah.

Gnosticism—the name given to religious currents in the ancient world that veered toward a dualistic worldview. Gnosticism was not limited to any particular religious tradition.

Hasid—a person of *ḥesed* (lovingkindness) and faithfulness. The word came to signify a person of pronounced spirituality, and with the appearance of hasidic communities in the latter part of the eighteenth century the term came to refer to the followers of a *tzaddik*.

Haskalah—the movement aspiring to bring European life and culture to Jews and to widen the intellectual horizons of Jews to include secular knowledge. After its earlier significant expressions in Central Europe, Haskalah made its way to Eastern Europe during the course of the nineteenth century.

hitbodedut—personal prayer and contemplation that takes place in a state of solitude; a key element among the followers of Rabbi Nahman of Bratslav in particular.

hitlahavut—enthusiasm; strong inner feeling.

ḥiyyut—the divine life-source and vitality; the élan that infuses all existence and makes existence possible. The *ḥiyyut* is present, though concealed within all that is. Since without *ḥiyyut*—the Divine Presence within all existence—nothing could be, in a more ultimate sense it can be said that God is the sole reality.

Holy Letters—letters of the Torah underlying all existence and thought to be instrumental in the Creation of the world.

homily—sermon. The hasidic homilies could have been delivered in a synagogue or in more formal settings, often at the traditional Third Meal on Shabbat afternoon.

Kabbalah—the major Jewish mystic tradition, which emerged (it is believed) in the late twelfth century, possibly in Provence.

kavvanah (plural: *kavvanot*)—intent, devotion; also, in Lurianic practice, designated statements to be recited with contemplation prior to performing certain mitzvot in order that those acts might then be effective in restoring the Divine Unity. The *kavvanot* were believed to enhance the effectiveness of those acts in restoring the Divine Unity.

kelipot—"shells"; the lower and evil realms of being, which, according to Lurianic Kabbalah, emerged with the Shattering of the Vessels.

king-mashal—rabbinic convention of parables employing a king-figure. A considerable number of king-parables are found in talmudic and midrashic literature.

Luria (Rabbi Isaac) and *Lurianic Kabbalah* (1534–1572)—in the last two years of his life Luria settled in Safed, where he became the foremost kabbalistic thinker and teacher in that intellectual and spiritual center. His thought had tremendous influence during the seventeenth and eighteenth centuries.

maggid—a term for an itinerant preacher and also for the position of preacher in a traditional Jewish community. "The Maggid" or "the great Maggid" became the standard way of referring to Dov Baer of Mezherich (d. 1772), who became the major teacher of Hasidism in the decade following the death of the Baal Shem Tov.

Maimonides—Moses ben Maimon, the *Rambam* (1135–1204); the foremost medieval Jewish philosopher. Though a wide chasm separates the rational Maimonides—influenced by Aristotle as the medieval Arab philosophers understood him—from both Kabbalah and Hasidism, certain terms and concepts accepted in hasidic thought can be traced to Maimonides and beyond him to Aristotelian philosophy.

mashal—parable; or the parable story itself apart from the accompanying explanation. A brief, imaginative narrative whose meaning is dependent upon a truth or situation beyond itself.

midrash; the Midrash—a rabbinic reading of a biblical verse, and also a voluminous literature comprised of such midrashic interpretations.

Mishnah—a basic crystallization and formulation of rabbinic law, the work of Judah ha-Nasi at the end of the second century C.E.; a systematic organization of the oral tradition. Both the Babylonian Talmud and the Jerusalem Talmud consist of discussions on the Mishnah in which the sages of the following centuries sought to elucidate its precise meaning.

mitnagdim—"opponents"; the name that came to refer to representatives of the traditional rabbinic camp that opposed Hasidism.

mitzvah (plural: *mitzvot*)—commandment or holy deed.

nimshal—a given explanation accompanying the parable story and an integral part of the parable as a literary unit.

nitzotzot—"sparks" of the Divine Light present within all that exists. With the Shattering of the Vessels some Divine Sparks fell into the depths and need to be lifted up and redeemed.

Other Side—(see *sitra aḥ'ra*)

parable—(see *mashal*)

rebbe—Yiddish term for the hasidic *tzaddik*.

sefirah (plural: *sefirot*)—in Kabbalah, the manifestations of the Divine Light, Energy, and Being, following an opening outward from the totally boundless and infinite state of the Divine.

Shabbat; the Seventh Day—a weekly holy day that begins prior to sundown on Friday and extends until dark on Saturday evening. A day of rest and prayer, of inner joy and tranquility as it represents a state of renewed oneness and wholeness extending to the highest realms of being.

Shattering of the Vessels—(see *shevirat ha-kelim*)

shefa—divine plenitude thought to descend and enrich this world in the wake of the spiritual attainment and illumination of a holy man.

Shekhinah—in earlier texts, Divine Presence or God's indwelling in the world; the word was employed in Kabbalah for *malkhut*, the tenth and lowest of the *sefirot*. A substantially feminine manifestation of the Divine Light, receiving and reflecting the light of the higher *sefirot*, the Shekhinah suggests a distancing from the infinite state of the Divine and the potential for disclosure, communication, and relationship.

shells—(see *kelipot*)

shevirat ha-kelim—Shattering of the Vessels; a catastrophe that caused the exile of the Divine, and a key concept of Lurianic Kabbalah. The vessels, themselves composed of Divine Light, could not contain the light itself, causing a collapse of the initial configuration of divine light and energy and the exile of its sparks into the depths, allowing for the shells to come into being.

simḥat beit ha-sho'evah—"the Joy of the Drawing" of water; a ceremony that took place during the Second Temple period in connection with the festival of Sukkot (booths) in the autumn.

sitra aḥ'ra—"the Other Side"; a designation for the evil, demonic reality that, in kabbalistic teaching, emerged with the Shattering of the Vessels and the accompanying exile of the Divine Life Sparks.

Sparks—(see *nitzotzot*)

Splitting of the Sea—the biblical tradition of the miracle at the Reed Sea, a crucial event and symbol of the Exodus from bondage in Egypt.

Sufism—the mystic tradition in Islam. Its adherents are referred to as Sufis.

Tannaim—the generations of sages during the first two centuries C.E. that led up to the editing of the Mishnah.

Tetragrammaton—the four-letter name of the Divine.

tikkun—repair or mending of the state of disrepair represented by the Shattering of the Vessels, according to Lurianic Kabbalah.

tzaddik—righteous; the term came to signify a holy man; with the social crystallization of Hasidism, it was applied to the leader and center of a hasidic community.

tzimtzum—"contraction"; in Lurianic Kabbalah, the withdrawal of the Infinite Godhead from a part of its unbounded self, making for a primordial space in which something outside the Infinite Divine could come into being.

World of Contraction (olam ha-tzimtzum)—the reality of the world that flows from the occurrence or perception of *tzimtzum* and hence can be experienced as separate and separable from God.

Yehudah ha-Levi—perhaps the most brilliant Hebrew poet in medieval Spain and author of a philosophical dialogue, the *Kuzari*.

yesh—concrete material being, contrasted with *ayin,* which is the divine substratum that allows for corporeal reality.

yeshivah—academy of advanced talmudic learning.

Zohar—a complex body of literature that appeared in late thirteenth-century Spain and over time came to be accepted as the basic text of Kabbalah.

Sources and Bibliography

〜

Texts from which the parables in this volume were taken:

Ahavat shalom (Ya'akov Kapel of Kosov). Lemberg [Ukraine], 1850; 1859.

Baal Shem Tov al ha-torah (Menahem Mendel of Gavartchov). Jerusalem, n.d.

Beit porat Yosef (Ya'akov Yosef of Polonnoye). Homilies on Exodus. Pietrokov [Poland], 1884. First edition, 1781.

(*Sefer*) *Darke hayyim* (Rafael ha-Levi Segal Tsimatbaum). Krakow, 1923.

Degel mahane Efrayim (Moshe Hayyim Efrayim of Sedilikov). Jerusalem, 1963. First edition, Korets [Ukraine], 1810.

Divre Menahem (Menahem Mendel of Rymanov). Included in *Sefarim kedoshim mitalmide Baal Shem Tov ha-kadosh* (Brooklyn, 1984). First printed, 1863.

Kedushat Levi (Levi Yitzhak of Berdichev). *Kedushat Levi ha-shalem*. Jerusalem, 1993. First edition, Slavuta [Ukraine], 1798.

Keter shem tov (Aharon Zevi ben Meir ha-kohen of Apt). Slavuta, 1868. Reprinted Tel Aviv, 1960. Lemberg [Ukraine], 1858. First edition, Zolkiew [Ukraine], 1794.

Likkute Moharan (Ostroy, 1806) and *Likkute Moharan tinyana* (Mogilev, Belarus; 1811) contain the *torot,* the discourses of Rabbi Nahman of Bratslav. Reprinted in numerous editions.

Likkute shoshanim (Pinhas of Korets). Lodz, 1924. First edition, Czernowitz [Ukraine], 1857.

Likkutim yekarim, a collection of homilies and homily fragments, largely the teachings of the Maggid, Dov Baer of Mezherich. Jerusalem, 1974. First edition, Lemberg [Ukraine], 1792.

Maggid devarav le-Ya'akov (the Maggid, Dov Baer of Mezherich). Edited by Rivka Schatz Uffenheimer. Jerusalem: Magnes Press, 1976. First printing, Korets [Ukraine], 1781.

Me'or einayim (Menahem Nahum of Chernobyl). Slavita [Ukraine], 1863.

No'am Elimekekh (Elimelekh of Lyzhansk). Jerusalem, 1992. First edition, Lvov [Ukraine], 1787.

Or ha-emet (the Maggid, Dov Baer of Mezherich). Hussiatin [Ukraine], 1899. Reprinted Brooklyn, 1960.

Or ha-me'ir (Ze'ev Wolff of Zhitomir). I–II, Ashdod [Israel], 1995. First edition, Korets [Ukraine], 1787.

Or torah, also known as *Rimze torah* (the Maggid, Dov Baer of Mezherich). Lublin [Poland], 1910.

Or Yitzhak (Yitzhak of Radvil). Jerusalem, 1961.

Sefer simhat Yisra'el (Simhah Bunam of Pryzucha). Pietrikov [Poland], 1910. Reprinted Jerusalem, 1981.

Shivhe Haran (Nahman of Bratslav). Jerusalem, 1961.

Shivhe Moharan, a book recounting aspects of the life and teachings of Rabbi Nahman of Bratslav. Printed together with *Hayye Moharan*, Jerusalem, 1962. First edition, Lemberg [Ukraine], 1874.

Sihot Haran (Nahman of Bratslav, included in *Shivhe Haran*).

Sod ehad dekri'at shema (Rabbi David of Malke'iv). Included in the volume *Hesed le-Avraham / mashmi'a shalom*. Jerusalem: Makhon sifre tzaddikim, 1995.

Toledot Ya'akov Yosef (Ya'akov Yosef of Polonnoye). Jerusalem, 1973. First appeared in 1780; the very first hasidic text ever printed.

Turei zahav (Binyamin ben Aharon of Zalozetz). Jerusalem, 1989. First edition, Mogilev [Belarus], 1816.

Yosher divre emet (Meshullam Feibush Heller of Zbarazh). Jerusalem, 1974. First printed in *Likkutim yekarim*, Lemberg [Ukraine], 1792.

Other hasidic and traditional texts referred to in this work:

Ginat egoz (Yosef Gikatilla). 1274.

Hishtaphut ha-nefesh (Nahman of Bratslav). Jerusalem, 1978.

Hitgalut tzaddikim (Shelomo Gavriel Rosenthal). Warsaw, 1905. Edited by Gedalyah Nigal. Jerusalem: Carmel, 1996.

Kokhve or (Avraham Hazan). Jerusalem, 1961; 1987.

Likkute etzot (Nahman of Bratslav).

Ma'or va-shemesh (Kalman Kalonymus Epstein). Jerusalem, 1993. First edition,

Breslau [Poland], 1842.

Me'irat einayim (Yitzhak ben Shmuel of Acre). Jerusalem, 1975.

Midrash rivash tov (Leib Abraham). Kecskemet [Hungary], 1927.

Or ḥadash (the Maharal). Prague, 1600.

Or yesharim. Warsaw, 1924.

Otzar ha-ḥayyim (Yitzhak ben Shmuel of Acre). Ms. Guenzburg 775, fol. 103a, the Lenin Library, Moscow.

Pesikta derav Kahana. Edited by Solomon Buber. Lyck [Poland], 1868; New York, 1949.

Pesikta rabbati. Translated by William G. Braude. New Haven and London: Yale Judaica Series, Volume 18, I–II, 1968.

Ramban: Writings and Discourses (Nahmanides). Translated by Charles Chavel. New York, 1978.

Reshit ḥokhmah (Moshe ben Eliyahu deVadish). Venice, 1579.

Sefat emet (Yehudah Aryeh Lev of Gur). Jerusalem, n.d. English translation by Arthur Green, *The Language of Truth: The Torah Commentary of the Sefat Emet.* Philadelphia: Jewish Publication Society, 1998.

Sha'ar ha-melekh: al mo'ade ha-shanah (Mordecai ben Shmuel of Vilkatsh). Zolkiev [Ukraine], 1774.

Shemu'ah tovah (Dov Baer of Mezherich). Warsaw, 1938.

Shivḥe ha-Besht, 1815. Edited by Shmuel Abba Horodetsky (Tel Aviv: Dvir, 1947); edited by Aryeh Rubenstein (Jerusalem: Rubin Mass, 1991). Translated by Dan Ben-Amos and Jerome Mintz. *In Praise of the Baal Shem Tov* (Bloomington: Indiana University Press, 1970).

Sifre devei rav. Edited by Meir Ish Shalom. Vienna, 1864.

Tanḥuma. Edited by Solomon Buber, 1885.

Tanya—Likkute amarim (Rabbi Shneur Zalman of Lyady). First edition, Slavuta [Ukraine], 1796–1797 (appeared anonymous). Numerous editions.

Scholarly, secondary, and comparative sources

Aarne, Antti. *The Types of the Folktale.* Translated by Stith Thompson. Helsinki: Suomalainen Tiedeakatemia Academia Scientiarum Fernica, 1929.

Agnon, Shmuel Yosef. *Yamim nora'im.* Jerusalem: Schocken, 1938; English translation, *Days of Awe.* New York: Schocken, 1948.

Armstrong, Karen, ed. *Visions of God: Four Medieval Mystics and their Writings*. New York, Toronto, London, Sydney, Auckland: Bantam Books, 1994.

Bergman, Samuel Hugo. *Faith and Reason: Modern Jewish Thought*. Translated and edited by Alfred Jospe. New York: Schocken Books, 1963.

Buber, Martin. *Or ha-ganuz: Sippure ḥasidim*. Jerusalem and Tel Aviv: Schocken, 1958.

Cirlot, Juan Eduardo. *A Dictionary of Symbols*. New York: Philosophical Library, Second Edition, 1971.

Corbett, Edward P.J. *Classical Rhetoric*. New York: Oxford University Press, 1965.

Dresner, Samuel H. *The Zaddik: The Doctrine of the Zaddik According to the Writings of Rabbi Ya'akov Yosef of Polnoy*. New York: Schocken, 1960.

Dubnow, Simon. *Toledot ha-ḥasidut*. Tel Aviv: Dvir, 1927.

Eliade, Mircea. *A History of Religious Ideas*. Chicago: University of Chicago Press, 1978.

Elior, Rachel. *The Paradoxical Ascent to God: The Kabbalistic Theosophy of Habad Hasidism*. Albany: State University of New York Press, 1993.

————. "Hasidism: Historical Continuity and Spiritual Change." Included in *Gershom Scholem's Major Trends in Jewish Mysticism Fifty Years After*. Edited by Peter Schafer and Joseph Dan. Tübingen, Germany: J.C.B. Mohr (Paul Siebeck), 1993, pp. 303–323.

Elstein, Yoav. "Margalit be-fi naḥash." *Jerusalem Studies in Jewish Folklore* 12–13 (1991–92), pp. 181–203.

The Encyclopedia of Religion. Edited by Mircea Eliade. New York: MacMillan Publishing Company, 1987.

Fainstein, Morris. "Gershom Scholem and Hasidism," *Journal of Jewish Studies* 38:2 (1987), pp. 221–233.

Fenton, Paul, ed. and trans. *The Treatise of the Pool (Al-Maqala al-Hawdiyya)*. Obadiah b. Abraham b. Moses Maimonides. London: The Octagon Press, 1981.

Fine, Lawrence. "The Contemplative Practice of *Yiḥudim* in Lurianic Kabbalah." *Jewish Spirituality II: From the Sixteenth-Century Revival to the Present*. Edited by Arthur Green. New York: Crossroad, 1987.

Frazer, James George. *The Golden Bough: A Study in Magic and Religion*. 12 vols. London: Macmillian, 1907–1915.

Gottlieb, Efrayim. "*Devekut* and Prophecy in *Otzar ha-ḥayyim* by Yitzhak ben Shmuel of Acre" [in Hebrew]. *Proceedings of the Fourth World Congress for*

Jewish Studies (1969), II, pp. 327–334.

Green, Arthur. "The *Zaddik* as *Axis Mundi* in Later Judaism." *Journal of the American Association of Religion* 45 (1977), pp. 327–347.

———. *Tormented Master: A Life of Rabbi Nahman of Bratslav*. Montgomery: University of Alabama Press, 1979.

———. "Hasidism: Discovery and Retreat," included in *The Other Side of God: A Polarity in World Religions*. Edited by Peter Berger. Garden City, N.J.: Anchor Books/Doubleday, 1981, pp. 104–130.

Gries, Zeev. *Sefer, sofer, ve-sippur be-reshit ha-hasidut*. Tel Aviv: ha-Kibbutz ha-Me'uhad, 1992.

Heinemann, Benno. *The Maggid of Dubno and His Parables*. New York: Feldheim, 1977.

Heschel, Abraham Joshua. *The Circle of the Baal Shem Tov: Studies in Hasidism*. Translated by Samuel H. Dresner. Chicago: University of Chicago Press, 1985.

Hisdai, Ya'akov. "*Eved ha-shem: be-doram shel avot ha-hasidut.*" *Zion* 47:3 (1982), pp. 253–292.

Hooke, Samuel Henry. *Myth and Ritual*. Oxford: Oxford University Press, 1933.

Idel, Moshe. *Kabbalah: New Perspectives*. New Haven and London: Yale University Press, 1988.

———. "Reification of Language in Jewish Mysticism," in *Mysticism and Language*. Edited by Steven Katz. New York and Oxford: Oxford University Press, 1992, pp. 42–79.

———. *Hasidism: Between Ecstasy and Magic*. Albany: State University of New York Press, 1995.

Jonas, Hans. *The Gnostic Religion*. Boston: Beacon Press, 1963.

Krassen, Miles. *Uniter of Heaven and Earth: Rabbi Meshullam Feibush Heller of Zbarazh and the Rise of Hasidism in Eastern Galicia*. Albany: State University of New York Press, 1998.

Lazarus-Yafeh, Hava. *Studies in Al-Ghazzali*. Jerusalem: Magnes Press, 1975.

Mahler, Raphael. *Hasidism and the Jewish Enlightenment: Their Confrontation in Galicia and Poland in the First Half of the Nineteenth Century*. Philadelphia: Jewish Publication Society, 1985.

Matt, Daniel. "*Ayin*: The Concept of Nothingness in Jewish Mysticism," in *The Problem of Pure Consciousness: Mysticism and Philosophy*. Edited by Robert Forman. Oxford: Oxford University Press, 1990, pp. 121–159.

Neuman (Noy), Dov. *Motif-Index of Talmudic-Midrashic Literature*. Ph.D. Dissertation, Indiana University, 1954.

Olrik, Axel. "Epic Laws of Folk Narative." Included in *The Study of Folklore*. Edited by Alan Dundes. Englewood Cliffs, N.J.: Prentice-Hall, 1965.

Pastner, Stephen and Rhonda Berger-Sofer. "*Rebbe* and *Pir:* Ideology, Action, and Personhood in Hasidism and Sufism." *Studies in Islamic and Judaic Traditions* II. Edited by William M. Brinner and Stephen David Ricks. Brown Judaic Studies. Atlanta: Scholars Press, 1989, pp. 113–137.

Patai, Raphael. *Man and Temple in Ancient Jewish Myth and Ritual*. New York: KTAV, 1967.

Piekarz, Mendel. *Bi-yeme tzemiḥat ha-ḥasidut*. Jerusalem: Bialik, 1978.

———. "*Radikalizm dati bi-yemei reshit hitpashtut shel ha-ḥasidut be-aspeklariat kitve rabi Tzvi Hirsh mi-Galina*," *Tarbiz* 54:1 (Oct.–Dec. 1984), pp. 263–288.

Polen, Nehemiah. *The Holy Fire: The Teachings of Rabbi Kalonymus Kalman Shapira, the Rebbe of the Warsaw Ghetto*. Northvale, N.J. and London: Jason Aronson, 1990.

Pope, Marvin. *Song of Songs: A New Translation with Introduction and Commentary*. The Anchor Bible. Garden City, N.J.: Doubleday, 1977.

Rapoport-Albert, Ada, ed. *Hasidism Reappraised*. London: Littman, 1996.

Rumi, Jalal al-Din. *More Tales from the Masnavi*. Translated and edited by Arthur John Arberry. London: George Allen and Unwin Ltd., 1963.

Sacred Books of the East. Delhi: Motilal Bamarsidass, 1966.

Sadan, Dov. "*Ha-otzar: le-darko shel mashal ve-nimshal*." *Maḥana'im* 46 (1960), pp. 116–124.

Schatz Uffenheimer, Rivka. *Hasidism as Mysticism: Quietistic Elements in Eighteenth Century Hasidic Thought*. Jerusalem: Magnes Press; Princeton: Princeton University Press, 1993.

Schimmel, Annemarie. *Mystic Dimensions of Islam*. Chapel Hill: University of North Carolina Press, 1975.

Scholem, Gershom. *Major Trends in Jewish Mysticism*. New York: Schocken, 1946.

———. "*Levush ha-neshamot ve-ḥaluka derabanan*." *Tarbiz* 24 (1955), pp. 290–306.

———. "A Note on a Kabbalistical Treatise on Contemplation." In *Mélanges offerts à Henry Corbin*. Edited by Seyyed Hossein Nasr. Tehran: McGill University Institute of Islamic Studies in Tehran, 1978, pp. 665–670.

———. *On the Mystical Shape of the Godhead: Basic Concepts in the Kabbalah*. New

York: Schocken, 1991.

Schweid, Eli. *Ha-Yaḥid: 'olamo shel A.D. Gordon.* Tel Aviv: Am Oved, 1970.

Shapiro, Avraham. *Or ha-ḥayyim be-yom ketanot. Mishnat A.D. Gordon u-mekoroteha be-kabbalah uve-ḥasidut.* Tel Aviv: Am Oved, 1996.

Silverman Weinreich, Beatrice, ed. *Yiddish Folktales.* Translated by Leonard Wolf. New York: Pantheon and YIVO, 1988.

Stern, David. *Parables in Midrash: Narrative and Exegesis in Rabbinic Literature.* Cambridge: Harvard University Press, 1991.

Thompson, Stith. *Motif-Index of Folk-Literature.* Bloomington and Indianapolis: Indiana University Press, 1955. Reprint, 1989. Volumes I–VI.

Tishby, Isaiah. *Mishnat ha-zohar.* Volume 1 (with Pinhas Lachover). Jerusalem: Mosad Bialik, 1949; volume 2. Jerusalem: Mosad Bialik, 1961.

Urbach, Ephraim E. *Ḥazal: emunot ve-de'ot.* Jerusalem: Magnes Press, 1969.

Wineman, Aryeh. *Beyond Appearances: Stories from the Kabbalistic Ethical Writings.* Philadelphia: Jewish Publication Society, 1988.

———. *Mystic Tales from the Zohar.* Philadelphia: Jewish Publication Society, 1997; Princeton, N.J.: Princeton University Press, 1998.

———. "On the Hasidic Parable." *Judaism* 45:3 (Summer, 1996), pp. 333–339.

———. "Parables and *Tsimtsum.*" *Prooftexts: A Journal of Jewish Literary History* 16:3 (September, 1996), pp. 293–300.

———. "Wedding-Feasts, Exiled Princes, and Hasidic Parable-Traditions." *Hebrew Studies* 40 (1999), pp. 191–216.

Yanon, Joseph. "Hashpa'ot tzufiot al ha-kabbalah be-Tzefat." *Maḥanayim*, No. 6, October, 1993, pp. 170–179.

Yellinek, Adolph. *Beitraege zur Geschichte der Kabbala.* Leipzig, 1852, pp. 45–47.

Zack, Berakha. "Rabbi Moshe Cordovero's Influence upon Hasidism" [in Hebrew]. *Eshel Be'er Sheva* III (1986), pp. 229–246.

———. "Rabbi Moshe Cordovero's Doctrine of *Tzimtzum*" [in Hebrew]. *Tarbiz* 58 (1989), pp. 207–237.

———. *Besha'are ha-kabbalah shel rabbi Moshe Cordovero.* Beersheba: Ben Gurion University Press, 1995.

Zimmer, Heinrich. *Philosophies of India.* New York: Bollingen Foundation, 1951.

CPSIA information can be obtained
at www.ICGtesting.com
Printed in the USA
LVHW091256270221
680110LV00001B/235

9 780827 607071